Warm Hand to Warm Hand

Warm Hand to Warm Hand

Dharma Writings from New IMC Teachers

Edited by Kim Allen and Kodo Conlin

Tranquil Books

Tranquil Books
108 Birch Street
Redwood City, CA 94062

ISBN 978-0-9845092-3-2

CONTENTS

Foreword

Gil Fronsdal
IMC Founding Teacher and Co-guiding Teacher

Our world needs to be changed in many ways for the welfare and benefit of all. But we will not be able to do this alone; it is a task we undertake together, in community and with the cooperation of many people. In 1990, what would eventually become the Insight Meditation Center (IMC) was a small group of about fifteen people gathering on Monday evenings to meditate together. Thirty-five years later, IMC is a vibrant community of hundreds in the Bay Area and thousands around the world. This year, we also celebrate the graduation of fifteen well-trained individuals from the first teacher-training program based at IMC. This marks a new beginning for our community that will ripple out to benefit the wider world.

The original fifteen people who gathered in 1990 laid the foundation for what IMC is today. Similarly, the fifteen new people who have completed their four-year training as teachers will help to sustain and expand our community for decades to come.

IMC was already fortunate to have nine wonderful Insight teachers, and with the addition of these new graduates we have nearly tripled our teaching capacity. Beyond this, more than fifty individuals contribute to our community through mentoring, facilitation, Dharma leadership, and Sangha leadership. Together, we form a dynamic, thriving community that will continue to grow in the future and to increase its positive impact on the world.

Buddhist practice is traditionally passed down from one generation to the next through personal contact, often referred to in the West as "warm hand to warm hand." I, too, learned from my own Buddhist teachers, particularly those who influenced me the most with their warm hands and hearts. I was deeply moved by who they were, how they lived, and the depth of their practice. What they taught through their words was important, but it was their actions, inner virtues, and inspiring character that truly shaped me as a person, as a practitioner, and as a teacher.

Now, Andrea Fella (IMC's Co-guiding Teacher) and I have the privilege of being inspired by the fifteen new teachers who have contributed chapters to this book. This book is a manifestation of Buddhism's warm-hand-to-warm-hand transmission. Andrea and I have met with the trainees almost monthly for the past four years, holding daylong or longer sessions to train, teach, and prepare them for their new role as teachers. More importantly, we have come to recognize that each of them embodies immense goodness, sincerity, and maturity in the Dharma. The Dharma flame has been passed to them, and now they have warm hands and bright hearts to share the Dharma with the world and to carry it forward to future generations.

This book serves as an introduction to these remarkable new teachers, for both the IMC community and beyond. They have much to offer, and I am confident that they will play an essential role in improving our world. May their wisdom, as expressed through this book, benefit us all.

Preface

Andrea Fella, IMC Co-guiding Teacher

Four years ago, as Gil Fronsdal and I began creating the curriculum for IMC's first teacher training, we placed a strong emphasis on learning by doing, including learning through collaborative projects.

In the final months of the training, Gil and I asked Vanessa Able, a Zen teacher and an author, to offer a writing workshop for our new teachers. As part of that workshop, they each wrote an essay on a Dharma topic of their choosing. Over the course of a few months, they drafted and revised their essays with Vanessa's support, and went through a peer review process with each other.

As the workshop progressed, Gil and I were so delighted with the essays that we decided to suggest a new project for the group: the creation of this book. While IMC offered the funding for publication, the new teachers themselves spearheaded the project: Kodo Conlin and Kim Allen served as general editors for the book, working with IMC's long-time volunteer editor Elena Silverman to design the book. David Lorey and Jan Lorey Hood offered a careful review of all the essays.

It has been such a privilege to train these fifteen new teachers over the last four years. We hope you will enjoy meeting them through their own words.

Simple Kindness

Shelley Gault

After all the years
what remains—
the kindness of strangers,

ordinary goodness,
a hand held out, a smile—

something to treasure,
something to aspire to.

Sometimes when people anticipate practicing metta, what we often translate as "loving-kindness," they set a very high bar for themselves, imagining that their hearts have to be bursting with unconditional love or they aren't somehow "doing metta" right. In the early texts the Buddha describes radiating this beautiful expression of the heart over the whole world, without limit, so that it pervades the entire cosmos. That's something quite wonderful to aspire to, having a heart so expansive its care can permeate the whole world. But I'd like to make a case for also recognizing the value of a more modest kind of metta, an everyday friendliness that we often take for granted.

I'm thinking of natural human kindness, the kind that the clerks at the checkout counter at Trader Joe's offer me (and seemingly everyone else in line) every time I come in. Often I'm wearing a name tag from the garden where I volunteer, and maybe they'll ask if the place is as beautiful as people say, and I'll invite them to visit and be amazed. And as the pizza dough slides across the sensor, they'll suggest I top my pizza with goat cheese and figs, their favorite, and ask what I plan to do with two fennel bulbs? I'll share about roasting them with cabbage and potatoes, and maybe I'll get a little advice about which seasonings the clerk would use. A simple exchange, smiles on both sides. I ask a bit about what's going on with them today, when do they get off work?

We are just a couple of humans existing together in this particular time and place. I think cordiality is maybe a good word for what passes between us. There is ease in it. If there was tension in me before the interaction, it tends to abate; my heart is more open, not guarded.

The first time I met my friend Stewart, he had come up to Santa Barbara from Los Angeles on the UCLA library bus, a service in the '70s that carried students from UCSB to the UCLA library and vice-versa. I was just 24, recently married to a friend of his, an academic much older than me. We'd invited Stewart to our house for an overnight stay after his library visit. He was an MD/PhD, recently discharged from the Army and doing a post-doctoral program at a big hospital in Los Angeles affiliated with the university. He got in my little VW bug, and before I'd even turned the key, he started asking questions about my life—not about my marriage to his friend, but about me, what I cared about, what I liked to do. He kept this up through the whole 20-minute drive up the winding mountain road through the chaparral to our house way above the town.

It struck me immediately that he was actually interested in my responses. He wasn't just being polite, and he wasn't trying to figure out why his distinguished friend had married this woman barely out of school. He was genuinely interested in getting to know another person. Over the years, I've seen him do the same thing with everyone he meets. He is interested in each person's humanness, in their particularity. He's universally cordial.

This feels like metta to me. This person's interest comes across as a kind of love. The word "cordial" comes from the Latin root "cor," meaning heart. It morphed into Middle English as the same word we use today, at first referring generally to those things which "pertain to" the heart, which are "of the heart." Friendliness, care, goodwill—words we often use as synonyms for metta. To be cordial is to be heartful, full of heart.

Sometimes we talk about mindful attention as a kind

of love, and I think when we speak of it this way, maybe we are pointing to something similar to my friend's cordial approach to other people. Interest, curiosity, openness—with no agenda driving the interest. It's friendly, it's kind, it doesn't claim some kind of special spiritual status. Ordinary human kindness, simple kindness. My sense is that it's a universal medicine, medicine for those who receive it, and medicine in the offering of it as well.

In a discourse in the early Buddhist texts the Buddha describes four ways that a person "embraces others." A translation reads, "What four? Giving, endearing speech, beneficent conduct, and impartiality." (AN 4.32) These four are described as being like "the linchpin of a rolling chariot" in regard to keeping healthy relationships going. Linchpins keep the wheels attached to the axle of the chariot—lose one and the wheel will at first wobble, and then very soon fall off, stopping progress and dumping the unfortunate passengers on the ground.

Though the sutta is not about cultivating metta, I think these four ways of behaving are all part of the simple human friendliness that I'm proposing is a valuable kind of metta. In even the most transient interactions with others, we can give our attention, speak with a friendly tone, be gracious, and not prejudge or interact with an agenda.

In many of our daily interactions, this is our default behavior. Expanding our capacity to offer an impartial, generous attitude in our interactions with others and the world is a simple and natural way of cultivating metta.

On a trip to a big city last year, riding in subway cars stuffed full with people, several times someone much younger than me stood up and offered me their seat, with a smile and a gesture, often without words. On the same trip, I dropped a sweater in the middle of a big square and didn't notice it was gone; then I heard a man's voice calling behind me, and then several voices joining in the calling. When I finally turned, wondering what the commotion was, there was a perfect stranger extending his arm to hand me my sweater, a smile on his face. Everyone was pleased—me, the man who picked it up, even others who had seen what happened and also tried to get my attention.

Those are the kind of events I remember most vividly about my visit to that city—brief, cordial interactions with people, characterized by a generosity of heart, by openness to another. They were medicine for my heart. And I can see the four ways of "embracing others" that the Buddha encouraged expressed in those almost momentary encounters: there was giving, and beneficent conduct, and impartiality, and even when there was no verbal speech, there was endearing communication—a smile, a gesture of the hand that meant, "Here, take this!"

We live in a world where the divisions between us are constantly being pointed out. We are always being reminded of who is good and who is not. But we are surrounded by evidence of pervasive ordinary goodness—our own, and others'. The cordiality—the heartfulness—that is a natural, spontaneous aspect of our interactions with those we cross paths with every day is like a precious jewel hiding in plain sight. We receive this everyday metta, and we spontaneously offer it ourselves, very often ignoring how it sweetens our days. Appreciate it, value it, let it grow.

Shelley Gault has been meditating since her college days in the 1960s, practicing and studying in the Buddhist Insight tradition since 2003, and has spent over three years cumulatively in silent retreat since then. She is grateful to have been a student of Gil Fronsdal since 2010. A spouse, mother, and grandmother, Shelley teaches in the Open Door Sangha in Santa Barbara, where she lives, and offers her service teaching and in other roles for IMC and the Insight Retreat Center (IRC). Literature, the arts, and connection to the natural world are rich sources of dharma teaching and understanding for her.

Of Deer, Squirrels, and Willow Trees: Metta as a Way of Life

Kim Allen

Driving along a country road after a morning of hiking, I rounded a bend and was brought to sharp attention by the rapid flashing of headlights from an oncoming car. As my mind searched in vain for a reason, the car whisked past. Then I saw it—a stately buck strolling across the road on its own agenda. I easily had time to stop, but perhaps would not have without the other person's signal.

The moments flowed on, the deer safely across the road, and I felt the emotional aftereffects. Most prominently, a rush of warmth for the care exhibited by the other driver—the uplift of being part of an act of anonymous beauty.

That person did not think carefully about what to do, did not plan out the flashing of the lights. There was the deer, my car rounding the bend, the concern to prevent harm, and a response to send that form of signal. Faster than ordinary thought, their mind brought forth this action. Although I can't know the actual mindstate of that driver, the situation reminds me of the integrated care-in-action that I know can come forth spontaneously in our finer moments. I'm also reminded of painful moments when it did not come forth.

In Dharma practice, we don't leave this up to chance; we cultivate certain wholesome or beautiful qualities so that they become a more integral part of our life and more likely to come forth when needed. One of these is metta, variously translated as lovingkindness, friendliness, or goodwill. Many of us learn metta practice as a series of well-wishing phrases applied methodically to categories of beings: from ourself to a benefactor, friend, neutral person, and difficult person. This formal process can establish and strengthen the intention of goodwill, and also stretch it into new territory. But this is not the only possibility for cultivating metta.

The full integration of this quality into action, speech, and thought takes deeper practice. Metta is one of a set of character traits (called parami) that apply specifically to a person walking the path to freedom. These qualities grow steadily through practice until they permeate many layers of our mind, heart, and even our body. Perfecting them is tantamount to full Awakening, but long before that, our mind can call them forth reliably. Metta parami is expressed through how we are in the world.

Our care for all beings, including ourselves, forms the basis for metta parami, a stance of non-harming and responsive kindness. At the appropriate moment, we will offer a friendly gesture, respectfully hold our tongue, ask if we can help, or perhaps flash the headlights to alert another driver of a deer. Although we can readily get on board with the idea of non-harming, it is not easy to let lovingkindness permeate our being, through and through. Consider this quote from Ajahn Sucitto's book on the parami:

> [W]hen we make the resolution of kindness, not just toward kittens on a nice day but even toward cockroaches on a bad day, when we include dictators and brutal maniacs, as well as all aspects of ourselves—then we're making metta into a perfection, a vast and transfiguring way of life.

It is about not only stately deer, but also less appealing creatures—including people whose actions are undeniably harmful. Even harder than this might be to include all aspects of ourselves, even those that make us cringe. All of it. Metta parami is a way of life, after all. And the promise of aiming our heart toward something this "vast"? It has the potential to transform us. We can discover that our heart extends beyond the bounds we may have placed on it and is more flexible and resilient than we have allowed.

But we don't start with vast; we start with here and now, with the gritty or humdrum things of everyday life.

My neighbor feeds the squirrels. It's sweet in a way, but too often I open the door to our shared entryway to find one of these wild rodents hovering just close enough that I worry it could bite me if it wanted to. Not to mention the stains accumulating on the concrete from their urine. I've learned to focus instead on his generosity and to appreciate the delight he takes in giving these creatures a treat.

The cultivation of metta is supported by learning to tune into the energetic sensations that flicker, ripple, or course through the body. Emotions and thoughts manifest as such sensations. When metta is developed on the cushion, we feel it directly as sensations of warmth, softness, uprightness, and a certain kind of dignified strength—like a willow tree whose furrowed trunk stands straight as the anchor for its gently swaying branches tipped with soft leaves that move in response to wind and rain.

Becoming a willow tree is not so easy. The thought of my neighbor and his squirrel-feeding might bring a tightening of the throat, a narrowing of attention, and a trip down a familiar pathway of self-justifying judgmental thoughts. Such reactive thoughts arise seemingly without choice, but there is still agency in my response. Only when I open to the discomfort I feel through this unkind mindset—and when I actively decide not to abide in such pain for myself—will the glimmer of goodwill begin to illuminate the strong trunk and swaying branches.

As this quality of lovingkindness or goodwill becomes more integrated, its gentle, responsive strength becomes the way we relate to many internal mindstates and other people in the world. Metta as a "way of life" means meeting our own anger, sadness, or agitation with clarity and kindness, neither resisting and judging them nor believing and collapsing into them. It also means meeting others, even those whose values differ from ours, with the calm forbearance of the willow tree, standing firm and centered while extending into the world with flexibility and grace.

The deep cultivation of metta as a character trait, a parami, comes with some cautions also. One danger of calling something "cultivation" is that we may start to measure it. Once we think we have a handle on what metta is about, we can begin to track our "progress," set goals, and compare ourselves to other people. Such measurement introduces inherent limitations into the process.

For instance, we may begin to identify with metta, seeing ourself as a kind person—or an unkind one. When we identify with even a good quality like lovingkindness, we stray from the path to freedom.

Or we may hold to an ideal and begin to criticize others

for not enacting metta in the way we think it should look. Is kindness invariably soft and affirming? I heard of a Dharma community that became disharmonious because one member tried to enforce a certain type of kindness, actively telling others when they did not live up to that standard.

Kindness and goodwill take myriad forms. When I was teaching meditation in the psychiatric unit of a hospital, I got to know one of the occupational therapists who worked with the patients regularly. She commented one day that she could see them attempting to care for each other, although that sometimes looked very unusual, such as reaching over to slap the table in front of a fellow patient who was crying. Such a gesture is not conventional kindness, but the sincerity behind it can still be seen and felt. We would do well not to limit our ideas of what metta can look like; the kindness that partakes of the path to freedom has nothing to do with measurement.

For metta to become a "vast and transfiguring way of life," as Sucitto puts it, we take each small moment and grant it its place in the whole. Without losing the ability to differentiate what is helpful and harmful—to clearly name "dictators and brutal maniacs," for instance—we broaden and soften our mind to encompass the fullness of experience. By tuning into the energies of the body, we discover how to stay grounded and firm while also swaying with the breezes of life, like the willow tree.

Ajahn Sucitto says of mature metta parami: "The result... is a mind that is grounded in wisdom and compassion, and which easily opens to the peace of Nibbana." May it be so.

Kim Allen has practiced in the IMC community for over 20 years, as well as in Asia and on long retreats. She helped create the Lay Contemplative form of practice that supports people living full lives of Dharma. Her teachings, collected at www.uncontrived.org, draw on her background in sutta study, inquiry, and the wish to foster the Dharma's unfolding in the West.

The Stinginess of Crows: Practicing Imperfectly the Perfections

Kodo Conlin

It might have been while sitting by the window, reading Acariya Dhammapala's *A Treatise on the Perfections* under a San Francisco sunset's purples and pinks, that I noticed a streak of black, then another. In those winter minutes when hundreds swept by to join their warm roost, I came to reflect on the stinginess of crows.

Unlike Buddhas, crows steal things. Hardly a model of generosity, a murder of crows is depicted in a story as distracting a river otter to make off with its caught fish. Crows are as clever as their raven cousins, who in Juneau in 1991 pilfered from a children's Easter egg hunt. "Almost 1,200 hard-boiled eggs were distributed throughout the Adair-Kennedy Memorial Park. Unfortunately, the staff and volunteers had distributed the eggs hours before the event. By the time they were through registering the attending children, ravens had already crashed the event and were making off with colored eggs in all directions."*

I can hardly fault corvids for not abiding by our social mores, despite their sophisticated communication and brilliant memories. I can't fault them, but these stories reminded me of my own tight-fistedness, when those palpable impulses toward stinginess arise: a grimace on my lip during a stressful conversation, a tension in the ribs while driving, an open hand of generosity becoming a closed fist. These impulses pull back, push away, grasp or push aside, so often when notions of "me" and "mine" dominate the mind, even while I aspire to a perfected generosity.

The stinginess I share with crows echoes my understanding of Dhammapala: that we practice the perfections imperfectly. In his language, the perfections (parami) are both "conduct" and "virtues." I understand this to mean the ten perfections are both practices and results. They are practiced, even clumsily, and they issue profound results, even to the point of Buddhahood. That the paramis are both practices and results means that I might practice imperfectly, even tentatively, good-enough-for-now, while orienting toward a mature, consummated virtue. Perhaps crows need not be perfect either.

In *A Treatise on the Perfections*, Dhammapala offers an insightful analysis and clear approach to practicing the perfections (parami), those ten qualities that are understood to flower in Awakening, their full maturity a necessary condition for Buddhahood. The ten practices: giving, ethical conduct, renunciation, wisdom, energy, patience, truthfulness, resolve, goodwill, and equanimity. For each perfection, Dhammapala includes concrete, here-and-now instructions.

Dhammapala's writings represent a fascinating period in the development of Theravada Buddhism. In India during the 5th–6th century CE, Dhammapala composed a number of commentaries on the ancient Canon, showing a sensitivity to other Buddhist traditions and providing a thoughtful, thorough consideration of ancient Buddhist practices. And while the aspirations he describes are second to none, the pragmatism of Dhammapala's approach includes that we practice imperfectly, which can inspire a sense of experimentation, even play.

Crows rarely glide, opting for a steady flight of rhythmic strokes. At the cliffs of Fort Funston at San Francisco's southwest limit, what I see is unexpected. Here, the winds are strong, continuous updrafts, fit for the humans in helmets and jumpers carrying their hang gliders to a cliffside launch pad. Surprisingly, the crows seem to have picked up on this form of play. Just beyond an arm's length from the cliff edge, a crow is suspended, seemingly stationary, wings wide, bones steady as a figure model, a swift updraft flickering the covert and flight feathers. This crow, suspended above sea spray by forces from across the Pacific, has me in exquisite wonder. With precision, she dives and somersaults below the cliff edge and back, disappearing and reappearing, still yet aloft. Diving and rising, this crow is not motivated now by food, shelter, prey, or tools, but by what? To my eyes, there is nothing this crow is trying to get, nothing it expects to gain. Could this be enjoyment? Fun? Play?

This crow's playful gliding, with no hint of stinginess, inspired me to consider the perfections as practices fit for experimentation and play rather than the pursuit of gain. Such a view undermines the burdens we might carry in relation to admonitions toward perfection. After all, they are called the perfections. How often do our own standards of perfection make actual practice seem insufficient? Instead, to play brings levity. Experimenting brings curiosity. Without devoting ourselves strictly to gain, but with the precision of this gliding crow, how might we play with the paramis? With this in mind, we can turn to some of Dhammapala's instructions, those on dana parami, the perfection of giving.

A precursor to playing with the paramis is suspending our self-judgment, to include rather than eschew our imperfections. Right from the start of his discussion of the first perfection, dana (giving), Dhammapala includes our imperfection, our stinginess, in what he calls the "method of reviewing." In short, in regard to each parami, this is "reviewing the danger in [the parami's] opposites and the benefit in their practice." For example, in the case of the perfection of giving, to review "the danger in non-relinquishing and the benefit in relinquishing. This is the method of reviewing."

Here, one of our tasks is to consider, "What is the danger or drawback of this stinginess?" For Dhammapala, possessiveness does us harm: our coveted possessions are unreliable, subject to loss. How we wince when our heirloom teacup shatters. Not only subject to loss, Dhammapala writes that our possessions are wanted by many, even sparking conflict and creating enemies. How many children and parents must have been frustrated at the ravens in Juneau, flying off with "my" Easter eggs?

In contrast, to give, to practice the perfection of dana, has the benefit of ridding us of those worries associated with possession, the stresses of teacups and Easter eggs. Accordingly, the person we give to is to be regarded as a helper, a cause for joy, a "best friend" because they make it possible for us to give away, and to be freed of, possessions. As Dhammapala says, a recipient of our gifts is "a companion helping me to remove my belongings from this world, which is blazing."

To play with the method of reviewing, we pause any demands of self-judgment and instead experiment with the instructions: "What makes giving workable? Who might I give to? How do I do it well and wisely?"

Dhammapala gives further instruction: ideally, we are not to practice dana when we expect something in return. He suggests that with compassion and appropriate skill, we might give whatever is needed to whomever needs it. One exception: we are not to give things that issue in affliction. After all, non-harming is a guiding principle here.

Instead of supporting affliction, one way we might benefit both ourselves and others is to give as a corrective, when greed for an object has become excessive. In such cases, Dhammapala's practice is to recognize the arising of stinginess, to ameliorate it, to seek out a proper recipient, and then to give.

The encouragement here is to give, but not only to give, but to practice giving. Give along with a precise reflection; give observing the effect. As you give, observe how possessiveness untangles and kinship coalesces. To sustain the practice as playful experimentation, it is incumbent upon us to observe and to refine our practice. We might carefully observe ourselves and others during the entire process of giving, from the time we first notice impulses toward stinginess or generosity, to when we assess what harm or benefit might arise, to when we decide to give, then the preparation of the gift, then during the giving, and after. Does joy arise? Clinging? Appreciation? Gratitude? Distraction? We might notice, for example, our inner states during this process to ensure, in Dhammapala's words, that our giving "does not become either conceited or obsequious in relation to the recipients." Or along with our mindfulness, we might employ the contemplation of impermanence, ensuring wisdom guards against clinging. Swiftly changing and without a constant core, our states can soar, dip, and fly.

How is it that we might glide in the practice, sense and catch the updrafts, playfully commit to a dive, turn upward, and sense our path? How do we play our way with the paramis? Our experimentation isn't random. We have teachings such as Dhammapala's with which to turn and glide. His instructions do not encourage an abstract, unmoored dana, but rather, to put this perfection into practice and to observe what happens, adjusting the practice and trying again, observing and refining further. This can be a precise yet playful experimentation. We reflect:

what drawbacks arise in this way of giving? What subtle opposites of dana cause me to lose the supportive updraft of generosity, falling toward the rocky shore? What benefits arise in this dana practice? What subtle supports are arising—the warm updrafts that carry the practice along at a dynamic glide? How can I mature this perfectly imperfect play with the perfections?

This reflective, playful, experimental approach to dana applies to the other paramis too. For example, how might a playful renunciation look? How can wisdom be matured through experimentation? Such an approach is not harsh or rigid, but supports the qualities that Dhammapala says are the basis of all of the paramis: compassion and skillful means.

It felt like skillful means and generosity when a crow engaged me, and I chose to play. Perched atop a wooden pole on Lily Alley, her head aligned with the height of my own as I sat at a window on the second story, she cawed. Perhaps inspired by the isolation of stay-at-home orders, I called back, mimicking. The crow turned toward me and responded, "Caw!" We continued in this way, call and response, until another surprise: she changed to another call (they have over twenty). I did my best to mimic, clumsily at first, but well enough that we stayed engaged.

Was she teaching me? Maybe, maybe not, but regardless, a patient crow permitted me to practice imperfectly. Though likely without the volition to teach me, this crow taught me calls. I did them imperfectly. I presented and the crow assessed. As I grew in skill with one call, my tutor moved on to the next. I felt the arising of a bond, companionship, relationship, and compassion. They say crows have demonstrated a memory for faces for up to 17 years. I hope she remembers me.

Kodo Conlin is a Dharma teacher grounded in both the Insight and Zen traditions. Ordained as a Soto Zen priest in 2015, he is also authorized to teach through IMC. Kodo has spent much of his adult life living and practicing in temples, monasteries, and Dharma centers. He currently serves as Co-Managing Director at Insight Retreat Center in Santa Cruz, CA, where he finds inspiration in retreat practice and the dedication of fellow practitioners.

*Bernd Heinrich, and Hainer Kober. *The Mind of the Raven: Investigations and Adventures with Wolf-Birds.* New York, Harper Perennial, 2009.

Living a Dhamma Life: An Exploration of the Noble Eightfold Path

Ying Chen

I saw an image some years ago that has stayed ingrained in my memory ever since. It's titled "The Eternal Journey of the Transmigration of Spirit and Consciousness." The artwork serves as a visual representation of the spiritual journey from delusion to enlightenment. The picture depicts a rainbow emerging from turbulent waters of life, ascending toward the eye of awakening on top of majestic mountains. In the lower half, dark clouds envelop the rainbow. However, as the rainbow ascends, the clouds dissipate, transforming into clear and then pink clouds. This visual progression mirrors an internal transformation within the mind and heart.

At the mountain peak, a radiating sun illuminates the whole world down below. From these heights, a mountain stream flows downward through forests, greens, and rocky terrains. As the water descends, it undergoes a transformation—the clear water becomes muddy. The small stream grows larger, forming wavy river currents, before finally merging with the vast ocean at the bottom of the illustration.

I was particularly intrigued by the word "eternal" used in the title. I couldn't help but wonder why it was called "eternal." If this journey is truly endless, then what's the point? Why would anyone undertake it? I found myself staring at the picture countless times. It began to seep into my consciousness and resonate within my inner being.

At times, I can feel my own life stream flowing through like this. There are moments of sunshine, clarity; and there are times of swimming in the troubled waters of life, finding my way to the ground. Maybe you have such feelings too. Just when we think everything seems just right, a serious diagnosis may come, or a significant loss rolls upon us, or an unexpected disaster emerges. Sometimes, we can spin in the eddies of life for a long time. At some point, we may ask: Is this how life is? Might there be another way?

There is a simile in the ancient Pali Canon Samyutta Nikaya (SN 3.25), where the Buddha spoke about the mountain rolling onto living beings from all directions. The rolling mountain refers to aging and death. I would add illness, climate crisis, and many other forms of difficulty that come with being human. The Buddha asked King Pasenadi that if the mountain were rolling in on him, what would he do? The King replied, "What else should be done but to live by the Dhamma?"

For a few decades now, I've made a conscious choice to

"live by the Dhamma" as best as I am able. Sometimes, the rainbow would arise and sunshine would come through. Other times, I would struggle to find ground. Through the Dhamma practice, walking the Dhamma path, more and more, when struggles happen I'm reminded, "Oh this is where the path emerges. The rainbow emerges from here, right where the struggle is." There is a Dhamma path that lives within us. It is possible to find it right where we are.

I don't know if I care so much about the "eternal" nature of the "journey" any more. The path is the path. It's eternally a path. Is that not enough? I sometimes ask myself, "Which is better, endlessly spinning in the troubled waters or walking a path?" The answer seems pretty clear. There is a kind of mystery, timelessness, and peace being on this eternal journey. My mind and heart can soften into the journey. I don't know why. They just do. This journey feels like the nature of the practice. It doesn't matter how long it takes to practice. It matters that there is a practice path available to us, and we can choose to walk it or not, right here and now.

These days, the Dhamma path feels like life itself. It vibrates in the body, mind, and heart. It has aliveness in this body. The path fills life, limbs, muscles, bones, hearts, and minds. It fills the pores and cells, and changes the inner biochemistry and inner energetic field. How does the path want to express itself in the movements in life? How does it want to express itself now, in this moment, as words flowing through my finger tips? I pause for a moment, feeling the vastness within. There is the quiet Samadhi (concentration) here, available, recognizable; and yes, Sati (mindfulness), beautiful presence; and Viriya (effort). I find myself mentally capitalizing these letters, like they mean something. There is a kind of power to them. Yes. This Viriya—energetic, alive, infusing the whole being with vitality.

Samadhi, Sati, and Viriya are three aspects of the Dhamma path based on the ancient teachings. They are like the underlying energy of a Dhamma life itself. The totality of the Dhamma path is said to be eight-fold. It's called the Noble Eightfold Path. Three other aspects of the path are called Sammaajiva (wise livelihood), Sammavaca (wise speech), and Sammakammanta (wise action). These three aspects together fill the dynamic expressions of life based on the underlying energy of Samadhi, Sati, and Viriya. It's like when the roots of the flowers are well nourished, flowers naturally blossom. When our hearts and minds are nourished by Samadhi, Sati, and Viriya, their expressions in embodied action, speech, and how we live our lives will naturally be filled with beauty and clarity.

Sammaajiva points to a kind of living wisely, wholly. Like the mountain stream in the picture. The life stream flows in this world, without getting muddied by picking up dust, the unwholesome reactive tendencies, driven by greed, hatred, and delusion. A line in the illustration points to the Buddha's life, which doesn't go down to the troubled waters. The line curves up from the clear high mountain stream to the eye of awakening. The high mountain is lit up by the sunshine. The Buddha lived a wakeful life filled with the light of wisdom and compassion. This is possible.

Living a Dhamma life, we consciously choose not to cause harm as best as we are able. We sincerely practice living this way. Of course, we will trip and fall into habit patterns many times, but this is why it is a practice. We always have an opportunity to return to the practice when we recognize that we have fallen off the path. We don't have to add more harm by blaming and shaming ourselves or others.

When we are on the practice path, wise speech and wise action may be a joyous, vibrant, and creative force emerging from the gathered and collected inner field.

Wise speech and actions allow us to connect, to relate, to care for ourselves and for others.

Actions don't have to lead to glory or defeat, winning or losing. Instead, they can express a kind of dance of life through our bodies, minds, and hearts. Words don't need to have the destination of a book or a talk, or to define who we are. They are the streams that touch each other and soothe each other. They have a potential to enliven and enrich our own lives and the lives of others, and they can be the force to bring harmony and well-being. Together, these three—wise living, wise speech, and wise action—form a beautiful, alive force of nature in this world. Can you feel the aliveness right here?

The other two aspects of the Eightfold Path are called Sammaditthi (wise view) and Sammasankappa (wise aspiration). From one perspective, they are something emerging out of living with the other six aspects of the path, like the rising sun at the mountaintop of the illustration. They shed light onto the whole world. There is clarity and vividness in the mind and heart. It's like the high mountain stream flowing in the world without losing its clearness and purity.

From another perspective, these two aspects also are initial and ongoing refined understandings that guide and orient our heart and mind to what really matters in life, like what King Pasenadi said, "to live by the Dhamma" in the face of a rolling mountain of challenges. These two are like the rainbow rising from the dark clouds toward the eye of awakening. They inspire us to honor the full potential of being human.

This inner orientation is both the end and the beginning of the path. The path is often depicted as a circular wheel. Wise views and wise aspirations emerge from the other aspects of the path, and they also guide this beautiful force of nature, i.e., life, to flow in ever more wholesome and freeing ways.

At this moment, the "eternal journey" feels whole and alive. The Dhamma path fills life, through its flesh, bones, hearts, and minds, connecting inside out, with everything. There is a sense of awe and wonder to it. And the wandering mind wanders, imagines.... But where are you going, wandering mind? Do you want to miss life? Life doesn't have to feel like survival or dream. You have to live it.

Ying Chen has been practicing at IMC since 2005 and is part of the IRC teacher-training program (2021–25). As a wife, mother, and lay practitioner, she finds delight and inspiration in the potential for freedom and well-being in everyday life. Ying primarily teaches at IMC, IRC, and Dharma Ground.

Walking the Dharma Path: Lessons from the Yucatán

Johnathan Woodside

There are times during meditation practice when the conditions feel perfect, the mind is present, collected, bright, and at ease. It's like enjoying a beautiful day where the sights are new and fresh, the weather is ideal, and you couldn't imagine wishing for anything to be different. But meditation practice, just like the weather, always changes.

The last time I experienced a day like that, I was part of a small walking tour exploring the archaeological sites of the Yucatán Peninsula. The tropical sun bathed everything in a golden hue. The limestone blocks of the ruins we visited were said to have been cut by hand and, with great effort, moved to form the pyramids, temples, altars, plazas, stairs, causeways, and other structures. The bright sun, casting rich, cool shadows among the limestone, added to the mystery of the tour.

Then, in a moment—perhaps much like a deep meditation practice—I found myself straying from the tour. I remember hearing the tour guide's directions and thinking to myself, *I can catch up in a moment; let me just take a closer look at these bas-reliefs in the limestone.*

I found the ancient Mayan symbols carved into the stone so enchanting. They depicted symbols and mythological scenes of sun gods and rituals, rulers and warriors, creatures, and cosmic events. The desirable imagery captured my imagination in such an awe-inspiring way that I felt as though I had been suddenly transported from the present day into a magical age of the vibrant Maya civilization, where I fancied myself an elite noble charged with overseeing the architectural construction of a temple designed to track the celestial cycles of the sun, moon, and stars. I'm not sure how long I entertained these visions; it seemed like only seconds.

Then, the attraction suddenly shifted to a fear of the consequences of this immersion in a world so deeply spiritual and ritualistic. My imagination, tempted by the thrilling otherworldly connection to such a holistic ethos, was now thrust into the unpleasant realization that this uniquely attractive society came with its religious ceremonies and offerings, its rituals and myths, and its challenges and hardships. I found myself irritated by the realization and completely averse to the idea of giving up modern life with all the amenities I'd come to enjoy. I was certain that the pleasant fiction I was envisioning would be a far cry from the reality of what would likely be a dangerous and complicated life.

I managed to settle myself and took a seat on a shaded limestone slab, indulging further in my daydream. A thought crossed my mind: *Maybe there could be a way to live in this beautiful place, here and now?* What would it be like to buy land in Mexico, to buy a place near the ocean and embrace a new life inspired by the art of the Yucatán while enjoying the comforts of modern times?

My imagination conjured a secluded house overlooking a tropical canopy of trees that stretched out to meet the azure sea. I sank deeply into the pleasant occupation of decorating my cozy home with colorful, ornate headpieces, obsidian artifacts, murals of celestial jade jaguars, and cyclopean towers adorned with carvings of divine serpents. Everything I designed was key to my perpetual satisfaction and comfort. My fantasy of independent ease became more alluring as I lazily embellished the impossible. If not for a polite sense of decorum, I might have taken a nap in the shade that cloaked the limestone slab.

However, I slowly returned from my daydream, lucidity washing over me as I quickly realized that I had completely fallen behind my tour group and was on the verge of being overtaken by another. I looked around to get my bearings and tried to orient myself to the direction my group had taken. I was overwhelmed by a flood of excitement and worry. *How foolish I have been to lose track of them!* It felt like guesswork as I flirted with various directions out of the clearing I found myself in. I raced along the path, anxious at the idea of losing my tour group and missing the bus ride back to the resort.

As I rounded a bend in the path that followed a towering limestone wall, I caught sight of a group I thought was mine. My initial relief quickly faded as I drew closer and realized it wasn't them—I had fallen even further behind than I'd imagined. Taking no chances, I broke into a run, desperate to be reunited with the familiar comfort of my group. Anxiety and worry gnawed at me.

Then, like an oasis, I spotted a group of people I seemed to recognize. A man wearing a wide-brimmed hat and a lightweight button-up shirt patterned with red tropical flowers caught my eye, along with his wife's ocean-blue blouse and white capri pants.

I rejoined the group, and my pulse began to settle as my racing heart sighed with relief. A sense of certainty washed over me when I spotted the tour guide—a short, stocky man with sun-weathered skin and sharp brown eyes that seemed to take in everything. His unassuming clothes blended with the surroundings, but the blue roped lanyard around his neck and the small leather satchel slung over his shoulder made him stand out.

I realized I had found my group just in time, as we were preparing to return to the Visitor Center. The bus parking area was a vibrant scene, filled with a kaleidoscope of buses, each adorned with colorful mascots catering to tourists. The heat radiated from the paved lot, and I felt immense gratitude as I stepped onto our air-conditioned bus.

I took a seat near the front and casually watched my fellow tourists board the massive bus. I saw the familiar husband and wife, our tour guide, a small family with two children, and another couple—then another. But the more people I saw up close as they boarded, the more my familiarity and certainty began to waver. I glanced at the tour guide again. *Is he really the same man we arrived with?* I looked at the husband and wife—*Were they the right people or just stereotypical tourists?*

I began to doubt myself: Had I run past my group and accidentally joined the wrong one? All these buses looked so similar in their wild attempts to stand out. *Am I with the wrong group? Am I on the wrong bus?*

I stood up and looked around, thinking I recognized another family, particularly a grandmother, but I couldn't be sure. I felt silly yet couldn't risk taking the wrong bus to the wrong resort. Not wanting to appear foolish, I scanned the bus again, but it was no use. I just didn't know. *Should I stay on this bus or get off and search for a more familiar group?*

I berated myself for not paying closer attention earlier that morning when the trip began. I needed objectivity—I needed to ask the guide. Sighing in frustration, I finally conceded and approached the tour guide, bombarding him with a barrage of questions. With kind understanding, he reassured me that I was indeed with the correct group and moments away from departing for my resort.

Reflecting on this experience, I realized how easily the mind can become ensnared by doubt, restlessness, and craving for certainty—an inner turmoil not unlike the mental patterns we encounter in meditation. My travel story illustrates the five classic hindrances in meditation practice: Sensual Desire, Ill Will, Sloth and Torpor, Restlessness and Worry, and Doubt. These hindrances often arise in daily life, particularly during moments of uncertainty or distraction. Just as a pleasant day can be disrupted by unexpected challenges, so too can our meditation practice be hijacked by these mental obstacles. With consistent practice, we can train the mind to recognize these hindrances, work with them skillfully, and apply their antidotes to foster greater clarity and ease.

When we consider the antidotes to these hindrances, the arousing of wholesome mental factors has already begun. Our intention to meet the distracted mind caught in these fetters with mindfulness marks the first step toward liberation.

Sensual desire scatters the mind, pulling it toward external objects of pleasure, as seen when my attention strayed toward the enticing imagery of the Mayan ruins. Concentration restores focus, calming the restless craving.

Aversion stirs irritation and ill will, constricting the mind, much like my annoyance at the idea of giving up modern comforts. Rapture, an uplifting and joyful state, counters aversion by expanding the heart and fostering a sense of well-being.

Sloth and torpor dull the mind, leading to stagnation, which crept in during my daydream and thought of napping on the shaded limestone slab. Directed thought, or aim, energizes and sharpens mental clarity, breaking through lethargy.

Restlessness agitates the mind with overthinking and worry, as when I realized I had fallen far behind my group. Happiness or comfort soothes this turbulence, bringing ease and stability.

Finally, doubt destabilizes the mind with uncertainty, mirrored in my hesitation about being in the right place. Continuous attention, or sustained investigation, grounds us in direct experience, dissolving doubt and fostering confidence in the practice.

While this story doesn't illustrate the direct application of these antidotes during my walking tour of the Yucatán Peninsula, we find that with a mature practice, applying them to the hindrances will enrich not only our meditation but also our daily life. The Dharma path leads to the cessation of suffering and the realization of true freedom. It's a joyful journey of letting go, freeing ourselves from clinging, and uprooting the causes of dissatisfaction. May the many walking tours we take through this life be filled with ease and deep insight, and may we forever find ourselves on the right bus.

Johnathan Woodside is an Insight Meditation teacher offering Dharma instruction rooted in the Theravada tradition of ethics, concentration, and wisdom. Johnathan has been teaching since 2011 and is the guiding teacher of Mindfulness Outreach Initiative in Omaha, Nebraska, and Dallas Insight Sangha in Dallas, Texas.

Fruit of Practice: Wise Samadhi in the Noble Eightfold Path

David Lorey

The aim of this essay is to help decode and demystify samadhi, the eighth factor of the Buddha's noble eightfold path. We can accomplish this twin aim by recognizing the samadhi already at work in our meditation, broadening our understanding of what samadhi means, contextualizing it as the result of certain supporting practice conditions, and highlighting its role as a means to an end.

I would suggest at the outset that the majority of regular, dedicated practitioners already know quite a bit about samadhi. We are familiar with it in our practices. Not uncommonly, however, we are unaware that the stillness, ease, openness, clarity, collectedness, or grounded-ness of mind in meditation is what samadhi is all about, and that any degree of those states provides benefit and lends momentum to the practice. Often, we find ourselves seeking something else, something different, something we have read about or heard referred to in sometimes mysterious or misleading language. In seeking something on the far horizon, we may fail to see what's already present and already providing benefit in the practice.

Samadhi is not like some distant, foreign land where you don't speak the language or recognize the landscape. It's more like something familiar and close at hand—more like an orange, say, something immediately understandable on its own terms in the here and now of experience. Someone may have attempted to describe this orange to you—its color, the bitterness of the peel and pith, the sweetness of the inner flesh—but when you experience it for yourself, you know what it is, unencumbered by previous assumptions, expectations, or preferences. Upon knowing the orange for yourself, it's no longer necessary to define it, seek it, or even name it; it can just be enjoyed, and its wholesome qualities can be relied upon to nourish and nurture.

A benefit of this orange metaphor is that samadhi is a fruit of practice. We practitioners provide conditions, importantly the two foregoing path factors of wise effort and wise mindfulness, for the cultivation and care of this eighth path factor. Many early texts and teachings hold samadhi lightly, allowing it to arise organically instead of requiring hard work to make it appear. It is noted at SN 45.1, for example, that "for one of wise effort, wise mindfulness springs up. For one of wise mindfulness, wise samadhi springs up." Wise samadhi, nurtured by appropriate practice conditions, blossoms and fruits—springs up—by itself. And this fruit—connectedness of mind with contentment and calm—in turn nurtures the practice by supporting the arising of clear seeing.

A good definition of samadhi, relying on its etymology, would be "connectedness of mind." To this we might add, as IMC teacher Diana Clark has, a *collectedness* of mind that is accompanied by a feeling of well-being. This feeling of well-being is an important aspect of samadhi because well-being highlights the wholesome, pleasant quality of samadhi, something toward which to incline the mind, to lean into. Additional useful characterizations might include grounded-ness and goodness, stillness and ease, or quiet and contentment of the mind in meditation.

In a translation choice that has proven unfortunate for many contemporary practitioners, the term samadhi has frequently been glossed as "concentration," beginning when the Pali texts were first translated more than 100 years ago. At that time (and as early as the 1630s in English), the word "concentration" was most commonly used in a sense much closer to its Latin etymology, from *concenter* ("with, together" + centrum "center"), that is, the "action of bringing to a center; the act of collecting or combining into or about a central point" (from *The*

Online Etymology Dictionary). Beginning in the 1680s, the word "concentrate" was also used to mean distill, in the sense of condensing the essential qualities of something—perhaps in the way the juice of oranges can be condensed into an intensely flavorful concentrate from which juice can later be derived. Only toward the end of the 19th century does "concentrate" come to be used in the sense of voluntary continuous focusing of mental activity, to concentrate mental powers—the most common current connotation of the word. The earlier meanings echo prominently in the Pali Text Society's Pali English Dictionary, where samadhi is defined as "a concentrated, self-collected, intent state of mind and meditation which, concomitant with [wise] living, is a condition to the attainment of higher wisdom and [freedom]."

In a similar way, the definition of samadhi as being equivalent to the four jhanas (four states of progressively greater meditative depth) has overly narrowed our view of samadhi. This is particularly problematic in the case of the eightfold path, where this equivalence appears to have been introduced into the texts quite late in their development. Bhikkhu Analayo contends that, based on his research among the Pali discourses, the equivalence of wise samadhi with the four jhanas is found in only a very small number of instances. In contrast, many suttas list the eight path factors without defining wise samadhi in terms of the four jhanas. Rather than the association with specific meditative depths, it is the context of the other seven path factors that makes samadhi wise, that is, that makes the stillness, centered-ness, collectedness of mind in meditation skillful and useful.

Generally, and including for practice in the eightfold path, samadhi can be taken to be understood in the suttas as it is at SN 45.8 (and in the Chinese parallel, at SA 784): "What is wise samadhi? It is reckoned to be the establishing of the mind in the absence of distraction, it being firm, collected, tranquil, concentrated, mentally unified." While certainly the mind in meditation may find its way to well-defined states of depth, clarity, and equanimity, and while such states may number four or eight or various other numbers, wise samadhi can be cultivated in many forms. More important than distinct states is the gradual deepening of the meditation that brings ever great collectedness and ease, contentedness, balance, and equanimity. Whenever we rest contentedly in the collectedness, grounded-ness, wholeness, wholesomeness, and well-being of the mind in meditation that result from wise effort and wise mindfulness, we rest in wise samadhi.

So far then, we can broaden our sense of samadhi in two important ways: the term refers to a collected, still, grounded state of mind in meditation, accompanied by feelings of well-being and ease; in the context of the eightfold path, wise samadhi refers generally to the beauty and utility of meditative collectedness and ease in advancing the practice toward freedom.

In further broadening the focus on this eighth path factor, we highlight the utility of samadhi. For samadhi is a means to an end and not an end in itself: it's a fruit of practice to be sure, but it's a fruit that itself bears fruit. We rely on the cultivation of sufficient wise samadhi for seeing clearly: wise samadhi is wise, too, because it leads onward to deeper understanding. At DN 6, the Buddha says to Mahali: "[practitioners] don't lead the spiritual life under me for the sake of realizing [the] development of samadhi. There are other things that are finer, for the sake of which [practitioners] lead the spiritual life under me."

> The gradual training championed by the Buddha, one expression of which is the eightfold path, culminates in the meditative stillness and enjoyment of samadhi because this creates a field for clear seeing (insight). At the end of MN 39, a sutta that presents a detailed version of the gradual training, the Buddha uses a beau-

tiful simile to illustrate how a practitioner with a "well-samadhi-ed" mind in meditation sees clearly the nature of suffering and its ending:

> When the mind is samadhi-ed in this way—completely pure, completely clean, flawless, without defilement, malleable, workable, stable, and imperturbable—one ... understands suffering as it is; one understands the cause of suffering as it is; one understands the cessation of suffering as it is; one understands the practice which leads to the end of suffering as it is. [This clarity of seeing] is like a lake in a mountain range—transparent, clear, and undisturbed. Standing on the shore, a person with eyes could see oysters, shells, stones, pebbles, and fish moving about and holding still. That person would think, 'This is a transparent, clear, and undisturbed lake. Here there are oysters, shells, stones, pebbles, and fish moving about and holding still.' [I]n the same way, a [practitioner] understands 'This is suffering' ... 'This is the origin of suffering' ... 'This is the cessation of suffering' ... 'This is the practice that leads to the cessation of suffering.'

In this passage, we can see the pivotal place of wise samadhi in the practice, a place I would summarize as follows: *the still and happy mind of deep meditation—the "well samadhi-ed" mind—sees clearly.*

So, how might we practice to strengthen wise samadhi

in our meditation practice? The first and most important thing is to notice the gradual, gentle arising of stillness, collectedness, contentment, balance, clarity, and equanimity in meditation. Once such qualities are noticed, we should actively enjoy them, following the Buddha's injunction at MN 66 that the wholesome pleasure and zest of samadhi is to be cultivated. With these two modes of meeting the experience of samadhi—paying attention and enjoying—we strengthen this path factor. At each forking of the meditation path, we can further cultivate wise samadhi by leaning into, inclining the mind toward greater collectedness and ease. Similarly, we can notice clear-seeing when it happens: clear seeing of arising and passing, clear seeing of the tightening and loosening of suffering's knots, clear seeing of selfing, of attachment and clinging.

When we put samadhi to use in this way, we create a path to which we can return again and again. We don't have to wait for samadhi to become perfect to put it to good use. In fact, the practice encourages us to create the conditions for sufficient samadhi, *sufficient* for seeing clearly. If it supports seeing clearly, it's wise enough!

Of course, even the clear-seeing supported by wise samadhi isn't the end of the practice. Rather, wise samadhi and seeing clearly are wellsprings of awakened action,

action (and interaction) free from hindrance, unfettered and simple. In wise samadhi are found the seeds of this further fruit, of action in the world that draws upon a well-samadhi-ed mind: generous, big hearted, peaceful, creative, confident.

David Lorey began meditating as a teenager in the 1970s and then came to practice in the field of early Buddhadharma in the early 2000s. In sharing the Dharma, David is committed to helping others discover their own unique ways of using meditation and study to find relief from stress and release from suffering. Gil Fronsdal is David's guiding teacher; IMC is his home sangha.

Three Keys to Transformative Meditation: Simplicity, Gentleness, and Appreciation

Lienchi Tran

Imagine a serene garden, where the beauty lies not in the complexity of its design but in the simplicity of each flower, the gentle rustle of leaves in the breeze, and the appreciation of nature's quiet harmony. In this truly tranquil setting, we experience the profound effects of simplicity, gentleness, and appreciation—the three keys to transformative meditation.

Just as the garden thrives in its simplicity, our meditation practice flourishes when we strip away the unnecessary and embrace the present moment with a gentle heart. By cultivating a sense of appreciation for the moment of waking up and the subtle shifts within us, we unlock a deeper, more meaningful meditation experience. In this essay, we will explore how these three elements—simplicity, gentleness, and appreciation—can transform our meditation practice and lead us to a path of inner peace and clarity.

Simplicity: The Key to Clear Perception

Simplicity helps us avoid becoming entangled in what we observe, allowing us to attend to the unfolding of experiences in the present moment. The Satipatthana Sutta states: "...a monk knows when he is standing, 'I am standing;' he knows when he is sitting, 'I am sitting;' he knows when he is lying down, 'I am lying down'..." Just that much is all we need to do. This simple act of knowing what we know—without adding interpretations or judgments—anchors us in the present moment. For instance, right now, you know you are sitting, and you know that you are reading these words. This awareness is simple and clear, without complication or extra effort.

In the context of vipassana, simplicity means approaching meditation with a mind that allows you to be aware of whatever experiences are happening in the present moment. For example, when we are angry, we simply recognize that "there is anger," acknowledge that "angry mind is like this," or just note, "I am angry." Regardless of where we are in the practice, we acknowledge the truth of the presence of the angry mind; this is the experience we are having at the moment. It's just a humble knowing, a noticing of what's happening in the body and mind at this very moment. We do not need to change the experience by thinking, "I should not be angry" or judging it with thoughts like, "Anger is bad." If judgmental thoughts do arise, that's another experience to be aware of, such as noticing, "Judging mind is here" or "Thinking mind is here." Being straightforward in our approach helps us stay grounded and fully present. When we are attentive to our experiences in this way, we cultivate wholesome mental qualities—awareness and wisdom (noticing and discerning)—and restrain unwholesome ones such as aversion and attachments (judging and preoccupation).

The beauty of simplicity in vipassana practice is that it strips away the unnecessary layers of complexity that often cloud our perception. By embracing simplicity, we can cut through the noise and focus on the raw, unfiltered truth of our experiences. Practicing with simplicity helps us taste true freedom by letting go—seeing attachments and aversions for what they are, not as "ours," so that we engage each moment with a fresh, open mind.

Gentleness: Embracing Compassion and Non-judgment

Gentleness is another crucial principle in vipassana meditation, akin to the gentle warmth of morning sunlight. Sunlight shines on everything—high and low, hard and soft, beautiful and ugly—without preferences. Similarly, we practice with the same warm touch toward all our experiences. This means practicing with kindness and compassion for ourselves, no matter how challenging or pleasant our experiences may be.

Imagine we're sitting in meditation and find ourselves

repeatedly lost in thoughts, whether the same story or different ones. Despite our efforts to stay focused, we often find it difficult, which leads to frustration with our unruly thoughts. As a result, we feel like we're wasting time and become increasingly irritable. This irritation fuels our determination to try even harder, but the cycle continues, and we end up judging ourselves. However, if we change our approach to the relationship with this experience, the experience will change too. With gentleness, we remind ourselves that we've been thinking our entire lives, so the momentum of thinking is naturally strong. Since we haven't always been aware, our capacity for awareness might need time to catch up. We might also ask why we don't feel bothered by being aware of countless breaths. So why should we be troubled by countless thoughts? Just like our breaths, we can be aware of our thoughts in the same gentle, warm, accepting manner.

By observing with light, warm, and gentle awareness, we stay with things as they truly are, and our practice gains momentum throughout the day. This approach not only creates inner peace but also enhances our relationships with others. By being gentle with ourselves, we learn to extend the same compassion and understanding to those around us, creating a ripple effect of kindness and empathy.

Appreciation: Finding Joy in Cultivating Awareness

Regardless of how long we've been lost in our thoughts or busy with our lives, the moment we become aware is a moment of joy. This gratitude arises from recognizing that awareness itself is a valuable attainment. In vipassana, becoming mindful after a period of distraction is not seen as a failure but as a success. Every time we notice that we are lost in thought is a moment of gained awareness, much like finding lost money or car keys after a frantic search—the moment of discovery brings joy and relief, not upset and self-judgment. This shift in perspective encourages us to embrace every return to awareness with a sense of gladness and appreciation, no matter how fleeting the moment may be.

By reminding ourselves that our goal is to cultivate awareness—not any particular experience such as calmness, happiness, or insight—we naturally foster joy and appreciation for the presence of awareness. It's about being aware of whatever arises—be it pleasant, unpleasant, or neutral—without trying to control or change it. This generates a positive feedback loop that reinforces and strengthens our practice. This approach not only counteracts feelings of frustration or disappointment when we realize we've been distracted but also enhances our overall meditation experience. The joy of being aware, combined with a sense of gratitude, motivates us to continue our practice with enthusiasm and a light heart, making meditation more enjoyable and sustainable in the long run. Continuity is naturally developed through this joyful and appreciative approach, as it encourages us to return to our practice regularly. Each moment of awareness, no matter how brief, builds upon the previous ones, gradually creating a steady and enduring mindfulness. This ongoing process fosters a deeper connection with our inner experiences, leading to a more profound understanding.

Integrating Vipassana into Daily Activities

Beyond our formal sitting and walking meditation practice, integrating vipassana meditation into our daily activities can be a powerful way to grow our practice. By applying the principles of vipassana to everyday tasks, we cultivate continuous awareness and presence. For example, while washing dishes, we simply know what we can know, like the sensations of the water or the movements of our hands. When walking, we can rest our attention on whatever experiences are arising, like the feeling of our feet touching the ground or the breeze on our skin. While eating, we can be aware of the most dominant experience, like chewing. We can also be mindful of our feelings, whether we are enjoying the taste of our food or not.

Taking a few moments during the day to check in with our feelings helps ground the mind in the present and breaks the cycle of stress that tends to build up. By pausing to observe our emotional and mental states without judgment, we become more attuned to the subtle signs of stress as they arise. This proactive way of identifying and addressing potential stressors early on prevents them from accumulating and impacting our well-being. For example, during a busy workday, we might notice tension in our shoulders or feelings of impatience. By acknowledging these feelings early, we can take steps to alleviate them, such as relaxing or giving ourselves a moment of rest with attention on the breath or any available body sensation. This self-check-in practice helps us stay aware of our emotional landscape and to manage stress more effectively. This continuous, informal vipassana practice helps us navigate daily life with greater clarity, calmness, and equanimity, making even mundane activities part of our meditative practice.

By weaving vipassana into our daily activities, we turn every moment into an opportunity for mindfulness. The formal practice supports our daily life practice, and daily life practice, in turn, nurtures our formal practice, cultivating awareness and wisdom. This harmonious approach keeps us grounded and centered, even amid the hustle and bustle of everyday life.

Embracing Simplicity, Gentleness, and Gratitude for Transforming Daily Existence

Vipassana, with its emphasis on simplicity, gentleness, and appreciation, offers a path to a deeper and more fulfilling existence. Embracing simplicity allows us to be present without distractions, while gentleness develops a compassionate attitude toward our experiences. Appreciation further transforms our practice into a joyful and rewarding journey.

By cultivating these qualities, we enhance our meditation and enrich our daily lives. These three elements encourage mindful and intentional living, enhancing our well-being and supporting our journey toward liberation. Just as the serene garden flourishes, our meditation practice blossoms when we embrace simplicity, gentleness, and appreciation, guiding us toward a more enriched and meaningful life.

Born into a Mahayana Buddhist family in Vietnam, Lienchi Tran began meditating in Thay Thich Nhat Hanh's tradition before exploring Theravada Buddhism under Bhante Khippapanno. In 2003, Lienchi met Sayadaw

U Tejaniya, whose teachings deeply shaped her practice during many years of retreat at his monastery in Burma. Currently, Tran is undergoing teacher training with Gil Fronsdal and Andrea Fella at IMC/IRC and is dedicated to sharing the Dharma to ease suffering and inspire liberation.

The Direct Path: Finding Freedom

Marjolein Janssen

On one fine morning, approximately 2,600 years ago, the Buddha gathered with his followers in the market town of Kammasadhamma in ancient India. The townspeople, referred to as the Kurus, were known for their intellect and wisdom. The Buddha selected this location to share some of his most profound discourses, recognizing the Kurus' deep understanding of the Dhamma. One of these teachings continues to inspire practitioners worldwide: the Satipatthanasutta, the discourse on the Four Establishments of Mindfulness.

Looking out at the gathering of monks, nuns, and laypeople, the Buddha spoke:

> Practitioners, this is the direct path for the purification of beings, for the surmounting of sorrow and lamentation, for the disappearance of pain and grief, for the attainment of the true way, for the realization of Nibbana—namely, the four establishments of mindfulness. What are the four? One abides contemplating the body as a body, ardent, fully aware, and mindful, having put away covetousness and grief for the world. One abides contemplating feelings as feelings [...]. One abides contemplating mind-states as mind-states [...]. One abides

> contemplating mind-objects as mind-objects, ardent, fully aware, and mindful, having put away covetousness and grief for the world. (Majjhima Nikaya 10)

The Buddha promised the Kurus a direct path to the surmounting of sorrow and lamentation and the realization of true freedom from suffering—Nibbana. In the centuries that followed, generations of practitioners followed the instructions given by the Buddha in this discourse, with great success. The accounts of awakened beings that have survived through the centuries have been a true inspiration for many practitioners, including myself. I remember attending a retreat where the teacher shared a story of a monk in Thailand who was alive at that time and had successfully walked this direct path to complete freedom from suffering. He attained the final stage of awakening when, one day, his teacher suggested he practice until late at night. Staying up longer than usual, diligently meditating, the monk attained the peace of Nibbana. Hearing his story ignited a deep sense of faith in my heart: just like this monk, we all have the potential for complete freedom within us.

The Buddha's discourse to the Kurus all these centuries ago outlines this Direct Path. It encompasses the deeper teachings of what the Buddha calls *right mindfulness.*

Mindfulness, or sati in the Pali language, is an aspect of the mind that is present to observe and be with experience as it arises from moment to moment. The Buddhist scholar Rupert Gethin explains that this quality serves to guard or watch over the mind; as it strengthens, unwholesome states of mind diminish. As these unwholesome states weaken, we move closer to the goal of this Direct Path: complete freedom from suffering.

Through the cultivation of sati, my life has transformed, even though I have not yet reached the end goal. I believe I've become a kinder, more compassionate, and wiser person over my years on this path. Many others traveling the same journey have experienced similar changes. I've witnessed both students and Dharma friends release old patterns and conditioning, resulting in greater freedom and ease in their lives. Although it is referred to as the Direct Path, the journey unfolds gradually, with each step bringing new discoveries and breakthroughs. Small victories may arise in the form of staying present with challenging emotions, while larger transformations manifest in how we relate to ourselves and others—each are precious markers on this journey to complete freedom.

The Four Areas of Practice

How do we go about walking this path? What advice

did the Buddha give in his discourse to the Kurus? The Buddha spoke of four areas in our moment-to-moment experience where we can establish mindfulness. Let's examine these areas: the body, feeling tone, mind-states, and mind-objects.

The Body

The first area of which to be mindful of is the body. The body is a great place to start because it is directly knowable and always available to be observed with mindfulness.

One of the most common ways to establish mindfulness of the body is by paying attention to the breath. This is often how people start with meditation. Focusing on the breath has proven to be a simple yet effective method to bring attention to the present moment. For example, when you notice that your mind is scattered, you can use your breath to stabilize your focus. This practice involves concentrating on the in-breath and out-breath. You can focus on the air passing through your nostrils or, alternatively, the rising and falling of your belly or chest. Although it sounds simple, it can be challenging, as distractions often arise. When distractions occur—and they will—our goal is to gently return our attention to the breath.

Exploring the Whole Body

Another way to be mindful of the body is to pay attention to the overall bodily experience. I recommend doing a body scan, where you focus on each body part for a few seconds. Start with your feet and gradually move your attention up through your body, taking a few seconds with each part until you reach the top of your head. You can do this lying down, sitting, or even standing. I regularly use body scans. It often helps me to relax. I sometimes even use it when I try to fall asleep; it can be very calming. If you find yourself dozing off when you don't want to, try doing the scan in a more alert posture. For example, sit up if you are lying down or stand if you are sitting.

Feeling Tone

The second area we can be mindful of is feelings, sometimes referred to as feeling tones.

In this context, the Buddha is not referring to feelings in the usual sense; he is referring to a more specific concept: the mind's response to our experiences as pleasant, unpleasant, or neutral. This response is an automatic, involuntary reaction that accompanies every moment of experience. A pleasant response often leads to craving or greed, an unpleasant response leads to aversion, and a neutral response can lead to delusion. To become aware of feeling tone, we can ask ourselves: "Is this specific experience pleasant, unpleasant, or neutral?"

Sometimes, my cat can get a bit demanding when it's close to his feeding time. He starts to meow loudly and occasionally knocks things off tables or attacks the plants. I often feel annoyed during those moments. If I focus on the unpleasantness of that annoyance by reminding myself, "This is unpleasant," a little gap seems to arise between "me" and the annoyance. This gives me some breathing room and helps me to not be engulfed by the annoyance. I apply the same technique to pleasant experiences. For example, when I crave potato chips—which I enjoy but know are unhealthy—I acknowledge, "This feeling of craving is unpleasant." This awareness also creates a space that might be enough for me to resist acting on that craving. By practicing the teachings on feeling tone in this way, we can create that little gap that gives us the choice to act differently, supporting our journey toward freedom that the Buddha described when speaking to the Kurus.

Mind-States

In this third section, the Buddha encourages us to be mindful of mental states such as craving, aversion, and delusion, as well as their absence. The absence of these unwholesome states can be experienced as their opposites: generosity, kindness, and wisdom. According to Buddhist teachings, these various states of mind are the root of all other mental states. The first three states—craving, aversion, and delusion—are the roots of unwholesome emotions like compulsion, attachment, irritation, frustration, and confusion. Conversely, their opposites are the root of wholesome states such as compassion, joy, happiness, patience, and other such states. We can observe these states as they arise and pass away within our own minds. We don't need to become entangled in them; mindfulness allows us to witness them just as they are. When we notice ourselves becoming entangled—perhaps by pushing away feelings of aversion, or by craving more joy—we can shift our mindfulness to include the entanglement itself.

When I feel annoyed with my cat, I try to notice the unpleasantness of that emotion while also discerning the qualities of annoyance itself. I can sense tightness in my chest, tension in my forehead, and clenching in my jaws. Honestly recognizing these sensations of annoyance is very helpful; this awareness prevents the annoyance from controlling me, as it did before I started my journey toward freedom. Instead, I can be present with the annoyance. I neither act on it nor repress it. This practice can be applied to other mental states as well, such as craving, frustration, anger, and confusion. By simply recognizing the presence of these states and understanding how they manifest in the body, we can cultivate greater awareness and acceptance.

Mind-Objects

For the last establishment of mindfulness, the Buddha describes several lists of phenomena of which to be mindful. One of those lists is about being mindful of the presence and absence of the Five Hindrances: sensual desire; ill will; sloth and torpor; restlessness and worry; and doubt. The Buddha encourages us to observe how these hindrances arise, how they can be overcome, and how to prevent them from surfacing in the first place. Additionally, the Seven Factors of Awakening are mentioned: mindfulness, investigation, energy, joy, tranquility, concentration, and equanimity. Each of these factors can be cultivated through mindfulness. But don't worry about trying to hold everything in your mind at once. When the awakening factors or hindrances arise, simply recognize and be mindful of them. The Buddha also encourages us to examine the causes and conditions that led to the arising of these mind states and how different mind states fade away again.

When I notice the annoyance toward my cat, I recognize that this is part of the hindrance of aversion. The underlying cause for the hindrance may be my impatience with my cat or worry about my plants being attacked. The hindrance often diminishes if I patiently allow it to be present, without acting on it. Conversely, if I try to push away feelings of annoyance, sadness, or frustration, they tend to become more entrenched. Allowing and receiving these feelings is often what we need most. Throughout much of our lives, we have been conditioned to push away unpleasant states of mind, while all that was needed was to notice them and open to them.

Walking the Path All the Way

Over the years of my practice and teaching, I've witnessed that anyone can walk this Direct Path of mindfulness; it starts simply by taking one step. And then the next, and the next. Perhaps you have already started. If not, maybe you can start right now. To do this, in this very moment, pause for a moment and focus on your breath. Know the next in-breath and the next out-breath. And try it again: know the next in-breath and the next out-breath. That's all it takes. You have taken the first step on this Direct Path, just as the Kurus did 2,600 years ago in the presence of the Buddha. The scholar and monk Bhikkhu Bodhi states that there are only two mistakes one can make along this path: not starting and not going all the way. So now that we've all started on the path, may we walk this Direct Path all the way to complete freedom.

Marjolein Janssen (pronunciation "Mar-yo-line") has been practicing Insight meditation intensively across Europe, the US, and Myanmar, where she was ordained as a Buddhist nun. In her teachings, she aims to present a practical approach to Buddhist concepts and ideas. Marjolein teaches retreats in the US and Europe and serves as the Guiding Teacher at the Insight Meditation Community of Richmond, Virginia. She also teaches online events at IMC. For more information, visit her website at www.brightdharma.org.

Big Ears, Open Hearts: Receptive Listening Rooted in Mindfulness

Tanya Wiser

The bell rings in the meditation hall, inviting me to pause and feel embodied in the present moment. I feel the vibrations from the bell's sound reverberate in my body and sit silently until it slowly ceases ringing. In the absence of its sound, I imagine myself as a tree—still and receptive to silence. Sometimes, the absence of sound feels prolonged, and again, I think of trees: they do everything slowly, untroubled by time. Nearby, others shift quickly and rise from their seats while the bell still rings. I wait, imagining I have roots. The first hum of the bell is not the entire song.

My practice has taught me the value of staying with the full arising and passing of everything—from a bell to a thought, an emotion, or even an itch. Meditation reveals how quickly the mind wants to move on—often before fully attending to what still requires care. The mind and body are like the bell and the mallet that strikes the bell: the mind strikes, and the body reverberates. Like the bell, the body needs space and time to process the reverberations fully.

When I move at the frantic pace of my mind—like a striker striking too quickly—I often miss important details, make assumptions, and cling to my preferences. I aim to listen fully by experiencing sound, sensation, silence, and stillness. However, it is rarely easy to pause long enough to willingly receive life's more challenging moments.

I remember a time when I was suffering, crying, and struggling with feelings of overwhelm and inadequacy. I withdrew from the care and listening ear of someone I respected when they offered support. Instead of being open and receptive, I became trapped in shame and the overwhelming desire to disappear. I made assumptions about how that person would see me differently and more negatively and clung to how I wanted them to see me. Later, when I reconnected with them, they offered such genuine care and support that I immediately felt relief and all the shame I had been unnecessarily carrying dissolved.

One consequence of not fully attending to my experiences is that I end up replaying them, especially when I don't fully acknowledge or respond to something significant. These lingering experiences could be a moment that touched or inspired me or a time of suffering in myself or others. These moments can feel like ghosts: sometimes humming quietly in the background, or at other times rumbling around like small children demanding attention. Mindfulness enables us to recognize them and embrace them wisely. Sometimes, the experience of meeting things with mindfulness can feel vague or unclear. With reflection, I am able to articulate what it feels like in an intimate and non-conceptual way to meet experience with sustained attention.

This is a mindfulness practice called RAFT: Recognize, Allow, Feel, and Trust. This framework has helped me relate to experiences in a way that allows them to bloom or transform—helping me to release the little ghosts that pull on my attention.

The first step, Recognize, is like stepping into a clearing in the forest. We pause, listen, look around, and acknowledge what is present, whether it's an emotion, a sensation, or a thought. This act of recognition shines a gentle light on what might otherwise remain hidden in the undergrowth of our awareness. Naming and identifying what is here creates the foundation for a deeper connection.

Next, we move into Allowing, a stance of receptive openness, like how a tree accepts sunlight and rain without grasping or resisting. We create space for the experience to exist as it is, without judgment or interference. If resistance arises—perhaps a reluctance to face discomfort or an impulse to cling to something pleasant—we also name and allow that resistance. Allowing is not passive; it's an active choice to embrace life's unfolding.

Then comes Feeling, the heart of the practice, where we tune in to the sensations and emotions present in our body. Imagine the tree's roots sensing the soil's subtle changes—this is how we connect intimately with our inner lives. With patience and kind attention, we witness the natural ebb and flow of experience, observing how emotions and sensations shift, change, and transform when held with care. This step invites us into a deeper relationship with ourselves, enhancing our understanding and fostering inner harmony.

Finally, we arrive at Trust, a place of being available and receptive. Trusting our ability to be relaxed and open is simple, similar to trusting our body's capacity to digest food or the tree's quiet, natural capacity to grow and adapt through seasons of change. With time and repeated practice, we develop confidence that by being mindful, discerning, and caring, ease and clarity will arise naturally after listening fully.

I once heard a fable about the power of listening. A person walking in a forest heard a faint whisper calling their name. While their companions heard nothing, this person persisted, moving closer until they discovered the sound was coming from within a large boulder. Gently placing their hands on the rock, it broke open, revealing someone trapped inside.

This story serves as a reminder that genuine listening can help us remember and come back to what has been buried or neglected. At times, such as during transitions in our lives, we may leave parts of ourselves behind, only to find they patiently await when we stop, listen deeply, and reconnect with them mindfully.

Mindfulness is the process of cultivating clear awareness of the present moment by observing the mind with keen attention, balance, and receptiveness. It involves being fully present and free from covetousness (grasping for what we desire) and displeasure (resistance to what we dislike), allowing us to engage with the world as it is without judgment or distraction.

> They meditate observing an aspect of the mind—keen, aware, and mindful, rid of covetousness and displeasure for the world. (SN 47.40)

Like mindfulness, listening well requires me to be keenly aware and free of craving and aversion. When my mind is not preoccupied with its preferences, I can better listen to life free from reactivity. Mindfulness is a practice of opening my heart to embrace whatever arises from the external world and within. An example of the opposite of mindful listening is when I pay half-hearted attention while feeling impatient, comparing, judging, and then planning what I will say in response. Instead, when listening mindfully, I do so with all my faculties awake and attuned to the present moment as it unfolds.

To whole-heartedly listen means engaging the mind and body as collaborators. I attune to a speaker's body posture and voice—whether mine or someone else's—and grasp their nuances: the rise and fall of pressure, resistance, and emotional tone. Listening to everything, even the things I would rather not hear, is a challenge. Yet this is precisely what the Buddha urges us to do in our mindfulness practice.

> The language of the body is sensation, and feeling is the way we listen. —Kate Johnson*

The faculties of mind and body are interconnected, and the body communicates through sensations. The body does not conceptualize—its wisdom is beyond concept and duality. There is a natural wakefulness shifting with the flow of life and experience. By feeling these sensations, I gain insight into the more subtle, often unconscious, influences shaping my inner life.

The Buddha describes the path to freedom as the middle way, free from grasping and rejecting. Our hearts can keep loving when we are open, receptive, and willing to be touched by life's joys and sorrows. Our hearts withdraw and close when we resist, reject, and attempt to shut ourselves off from life's joys and sorrows. When I feel the urge to defend, move, speak, or react in response to challenging events, visitors, thoughts, or emotions, I invite myself to sit back and listen.

Many struggle to listen to all things equally, with balance. Yet we can look no further than our ears to find the balance to listen deeply and mindfully. Hear me out—pun intended.

Ears, like trees, are free from grasping and aversion. The ears sit quietly on the sides of our heads, perfectly placed to receive sounds from all directions: front, side, and rear. They are always open unless blocked by fingers, hands, or objects. They do not wrinkle like the nose when avoiding an unwelcome whiff, nor can they push out what has entered. Unlike the eyes, they cannot squeeze shut to stop incoming sense data. They never close like a fist, refusing to hold something. They do not shut or contract. The body may send fingers to block them, but the ears remain unchanged—steady, open, and receptive. They do not move to protect themselves or express preferences. They receive all sounds equally. Vibrated by what flows into and around them, they provide sense data crucial for connection, understanding, and response.

Have you ever wondered why the Buddha is often depicted with long earlobes that rest on his shoulders? They are prominently large, and I have pondered their significance. I can imagine his earlobes jiggling as he walked and vibrating as he chanted. In some Asian cultures, prominent ears are considered a sign of wisdom. Large ears also suggest an increased ability to listen with care and without preference.

Inspired by how ears receive all sounds equally, I drew the shape of an ear and noticed that it is almost the shape of half a heart. We have two; combine the two ears and form a whole heart. The Buddha had a remarkable ability to listen and respond to the suffering in the world with wisdom and compassion.

Perhaps the Buddha's elongated earlobes symbolize his

wisdom and profound capacity to hear everything compassionately. After all, wisdom and compassion are the two wings of awakening.

Finding stillness like a tree—rooted and receptive—can help us to stay attuned to the full range of life, including the quiet spaces between all things. We will discover that we have a profound capacity to meet life with discernment and kindheartedness. We will also become able to access a meeting with life that can be as natural and transformative as a tree taking in carbon monoxide and releasing oxygen.

As you finish reading, take a moment to sit quietly and listen—not only with your ears but with your heart, body, and entire being. What stirs within you? Imagine what might unfold in your practice, your heart, and your mind if you responded to life like ears, with listening and receptiveness, and like trees, with patience, rootedness, and a caring heart.

Tanya Wiser, LCSW SEP, teaches at IMC in Redwood City, CA. She works full-time as a mindfulness-based therapist, integrating her mindfulness, compassion, and somatic therapy training with insights from direct engagement with Buddhist teachings. Tanya draws from the teachings of her Western Theravada teachers, Gil Fronsdal and Andrea Fella, as well as Jack Kornfield, Tara Brach, and the

Burmese Monk Sayadaw U Tejaniya. As a white, queer mother and lay practitioner, she enjoys fostering a sense of sangha (spiritual community) within a relational framework of spiritual friendship, all while living a householder's life guided by a commitment to liberation.

*Kate Johnson (2021). *Radical friendship: Seven ways to love yourself and find your people in an unjust world.* Shambhala Publications.

Building Sanctuary Together

Liz Powell

I am writing this in solidarity to join our efforts on the Path in preserving an endangered species that is not on The Endangered Species List: the human race. "But there are about 8.2 billion living humans on earth," you say? Yes, and we are in danger of bringing about our own complete extinction.

Humanity poses existential threats to its own. Human-caused climate change has resulted in severe droughts affecting about 33 percent of the planet's surface. The UN Convention to Combat Desertification reports, "Around 40 percent of the Earth's land is currently degraded, which includes a significant portion of arable land being affected by desertification." This trend is expected to continue if we do not rectify the accelerating effects of global warming. TheWorldCounts.com website estimates that "by 2025, 1.8 billion people will experience absolute water scarcity, and two-thirds of the world will be living under water-stressed conditions."

With drought and crop failure, and the resulting economic failure, there follows persecution, human rights abuse, violence, and war erupting in many countries.

Millions of humans are fleeing these dangerous conditions, attempting to migrate. If they do not die on what are often hazardous journeys, they are being turned back at the borders to other countries, forced into desperate situations where they cannot go further and lack the resources to turn back.

Many more people lack the resources to attempt migration. This leaves an estimated "14 percent of world population ... within five kilometers of violent conflict," according to new data published by the University of Southampton. The Armed Conflict Location & Event Data Project estimates that over 170,000 people died in war and violent conflicts in 2023.

These are just a few of the life-threatening challenges humankind faces stemming from climate change. In addition, nine countries have nuclear weapons, a global nuclear stockpile of close to 13,000 weapons. Pollution is estimated to kill more than 9 million people annually. And then there are life-threatening events that are part of every life: illness, injury, natural disasters, societal and personal conflict. As individuals, groups, and societies, human beings experience mental, emotional, physical, economic, and social challenges of all levels, from the mild and manageable to the serious and difficult.

While we are faced with grave risks beyond our control, the most serious threats originate in human mental activity. Impulses of greed and clinging can have some people believing they will thrive by acquiring power and resources, which can lead to an impulse to grab more and more, no matter what the cost to other beings. The impact of poverty, illness, injury, and death can foster divisive attitudes between so-called "haves" and "have nots."

The human mind has the potential to contract in suffering: fear, aggression, sadness, and disgust at these challenges, succumbing to a life of misery. However, the human mind also has the capacity to turn mental experiences into growth and liberation from suffering.

We help turn the tide by making our practice of mindfulness a sanctuary. Each person embodying the benefits of mental sanctuary has the potential to serve as an example that influences others to do the same. A mind free of suffering spreads peace and rids the world of external and internal suffering, one mind at a time.

The sanctuary we can build is a place of refuge that offers safety from danger. The word refuge brings up images of a secure place that offers shelter from a natural disaster or a human-made disaster. In situations like those already described, the first refuge may be to care for the physical safety of those subjected to extreme events and hardships.

However, there are also internal threats from the human mind. We can create safety for the mind from various dangers. What are some of the dangers to the mind that humans experience? There is the danger of falling into reactivity instead of being able to respond skillfully to both external and internal events. The mind can delude itself into believing that it can or should control all circumstances to make crises work out the way one wants. It can also believe it can prevent or avoid any outcomes one does not want. The mind can falsely believe that one's happiness depends upon getting ourselves and others to think, speak, and behave according to one's views and practices. The mind can succumb to hindrances (lust, ill-will, lethargy and dullness, restlessness and worry, doubt in the Dharma, self-doubt) that lead to further suffering. In succumbing to these obstacles, the mind can swing between escaping into sense pleasures and giving up in despair.

What are some refuges from those dangers? Awareness in daily life, mindfulness meditation, reflective practices, and studying the dharma can each build sanctuary, creating safety for the mind. With mental refuge, when struggling arises with the external challenges, changes, and difficulties we face, one can clearly know that reactivity and afflictive mind states are present. When there is awareness of afflictive mind states, there is the potential to choose not to act out of them. When we don't take unwholesome actions, the mind does not feed dissatisfaction, stress, and suffering.

We cultivate a refuge, using mindfulness meditation and awareness in daily life, by continuing to apply ourselves to awareness of experience in the present moment. Often suffering is the result of the proliferation of emotional and mental upheaval based upon thoughts, speculation about the future, and rumination about the past. Awareness allows us to notice when those reactions are creating dissatisfaction, stress, and suffering and gives us the opportunity to keep returning to present-moment awareness.

Once awareness of the present moment is here, we are able to notice that experience itself is ever-changing and that reactivity is often based on rigid, unchanging, fixed concepts about it. We see that we don't have to act on what arises from those incorrect concepts, nor let them drive our behavior. There is safety in that awareness.

Returning the mind repeatedly to the present moment

also protects the mind from the unhelpful effects of "spinning" or obsessing on thoughts. We can safeguard it against emotional upheaval about how difficult or scary or anger-provoking or confusing a situation is.

In the present moment, we can feel sensations in the body that tend to arise with thoughts and emotions about the past and the imagined future. Noticing and being present with the impact on the body of this mental activity turns the mind away from thought-proliferation and emotional escalation so that it can calm and cultivate more wholesome options in the direction of more freedom from suffering.

A sanctuary is also a place that preserves, protects, and nourishes a resource. In a bird sanctuary, large flocks of birds of all kinds can find water to drink and bathe in, food to eat, a place to mate and hatch offspring, and a place for a brief stopover during a long migration—a place of rest.

We also cultivate mindful rest engaging in the Dharma. Doing so brings wisdom into one's life. We learn a wealth of skillful ways to rest, nourish, and protect the mind.

For example, practicing the Eightfold Path in concert with awareness allows us to respond to world crises from the wisdom contained in Wise View, Wise Intention, and Wise Action. Learning that actions have consequences, we become inspired to be clearly aware of our actions of thought, speech, and behavior. As we come to see that any of them are unwholesome, inclining toward suffering, we can decide to abandon the unwholesome action and maintain diligent mindfulness. We can watch for the earliest indicators of unwholesome intention and prevent it from arising again. In cases where mindfulness detects an already high level of reactivity to challenging circumstances, we can learn to cultivate enough restraint to respond with an absence of greed, an absence of ill-will, and an absence of harmfulness. These are far more restful approaches than when we are entangled in unwholesome behavior!

This points to our power to shape our attention and, therefore, our experience. By maintaining our attention to choices toward the generous, the moral, and the renunciate, we enjoy and create internal and external safety for ourselves and others. As others observe our well-being, they are inspired to find their way toward freedom as well.

A sanctuary is also a sacred place, apart from the profane or ordinary. We can treat the ways we practice and study the Dharma as the precious, extraordinary, rare resources that they are. We can devote ourselves to practice with the reverence we would accord the discovery of an ancient scroll containing the key to immortality. We can visit this sanctuary every day with the awe and enthusiasm of one given the only key to an ancient site of unsurpassed beauty that few are allowed to enter. We can find joy and ultimate peace in this sanctuary.

Knowing this is something we build together brings a sense of happiness and determination. Together, we can change the human mind, one mind at a time, and prevent the self-destruction of the human race.

Liz Powell has been practicing vipassana meditation since 2004. She is a grateful graduate of three dharma teacher-, leader-, and mentor-training programs offered between 2014 and 2025 by Gil Fronsdal and Andrea Fella, as well as the Dedicated Practitioners and Advanced Practitioners programs at Spirit Rock. She has offered programs at IMC for many years, including The Eightfold Path, Happy Hour brahmavihara practice, Intro courses, and half-day and daylong retreats (including many for children, families and parents). She has also served as IMC Board President and the Managing Director of IRC.

Cultivating Peace

Ari Crellin-Quick

The path to lasting happiness begins with understanding. One of the central themes of Buddhism is that everything arises naturally in dependence upon the causes and conditions that support it. Things don't arise randomly or come about just because we wish for them. For example, if we want an apple tree, we need to plant a seed in the earth and ensure it receives adequate water, sunlight, and nutrients. We may also need to provide protection to the vulnerable, tender sapling. It isn't our job to make the plant grow, but rather to tend to the conditions that allow for the unfolding of nature in the direction that we're wanting—namely, to give rise to a healthy and productive apple tree. However, if we don't first work to understand the causes and conditions that actually give rise to a productive apple tree, we may end up making great efforts that are completely ineffectual, and may even be at odds with our aim. For example, if we plant a seed in the earth, but dig it up every hour to check on its progress, it will not grow. So in order to effectively work with nature to yield the desired results, we first need to have some understanding of the laws and principles that govern its unfolding.

Likewise, in our quest for happiness, we need to start with an understanding of the actual causes and conditions that produce it in order for our endeavor to bear the desired fruit. With this understanding in place, we can more effectively direct our efforts toward establishing the conditions that naturally give rise to happiness, rather than—perhaps unwittingly—acting in ways that lead directly away from it.

The word Dharma, in addition to referring to the teachings of the Buddha, also refers to nature, and to the laws and principles that govern its unfolding. The Buddha's teachings are not concerned with the natural laws of physics or biology, but rather with the laws and principles that govern our experience of happiness on the one hand, and dukkha on the other. Dukkha, a Pali word, can be translated as stress, suffering, or dissatisfaction, and runs the gamut from subtle unease to abject suffering. The Buddha understood that we are all doing our best to minimize the amount of dukkha we experience, but because we usually misapprehend its true causes, many of our efforts simply end up creating more suffering in our lives and in the world around us. For example, we may feel that amassing resources or maximizing our enjoyment of sensual pleasures will make us happy or secure. In reality, these strategies give rise to greater tension and make us more fearfully dependent on things going our way.

Equipped with a greater understanding of how dukkha comes to an end, we can more effectively work with nature, as stewards of this natural process, without giving in to our habitual yet counterproductive attempts to force, control, or strain. An image the Buddha offers to illustrate this principle is that of a hen laying on her clutch of eggs. If she regularly incubates them and keeps them warm and protected, then her chicks will hatch safely. She does not need to wish, "May my chicks grow and hatch safely." But if she doesn't regularly incubate them, no amount of wishing will make them hatch. Likewise, if we continually develop wholesome or skillful qualities of mind—such as kindness, patience, compassion, letting go, and wise discernment—then our experience will naturally and inevitably move toward greater peace and freedom. This peace is simply the natural outcome of establishing the appropriate conditions that allow for it to arise; it isn't something that can be wished into existence or manifested through sheer willpower.

Deep and lasting happiness doesn't come all at once but emerges gradually, through continuous, moment-by-moment cultivation. The Buddha illustrated this with the analogy of the gradual wearing away of the wooden handle of a carpenter's frequently used tool: from day to day, the handle likely shows no discernible difference, but over time, after years of regular use, it is worn away such that it fits the shape of the user's hand.

Whatever we do, whether good or for ill—even the smallest act, intention, or movement of the heart—sets in motion a process that, when repeatedly fed, is capable of growing into something substantial with powerful momentum. Understanding the potential of each moment of how we are being in our lives—that is, what we're oriented toward, what qualities of mind we're acting out of, what we're focusing on—naturally gives rise to a deep sense of heedfulness or careful attention. We take great care with our intentions and lovingly guard our minds to shepherd this ever-unfolding process toward something that is truly beautiful and freeing. More and more, our hearts incline toward ethical integrity and peace rather than craving and agitation. Our natural resonance with this inner alignment—an immediate fruit of wholesome mind states—gives rise to a powerful, positive feedback loop. We naturally tend toward a way of being that supports—and is an expression of—a deeper kind of happiness.

We don't have to become perfect beings overnight—

nor can we. But in recognizing that everything we do contributes to our current and future happiness or suffering, we take care in each moment to simply aim in the direction of the wholesome and beneficial. And rather than demanding immediate results, we take heart in knowing that we're on the path and moving in the right direction. We take refuge in an approach that actually leads to peace, not continued bewilderment. How we live each moment of our lives—this moment, right here; and now this moment, here—sets the conditions that allow for the flowering of happiness to naturally unfold.

Ari Crellin-Quick has been a student of the Dharma since 2004. Having profoundly benefited from this practice, he is grateful to be able to support others through teaching and mentoring.

Ocean with Lighthouse: On Cultivating Equanimity

Dawn Neal

The lighthouse at my local harbor stands like a giant pillar overlooking the sea. Day or night, in blue skies or storms, it stands at the side of the ocean. Even on a quiet day, large waves wet it with silver and white foam. It is clearly solid; it remains stable in any form of weather. Equanimity is like this too: steady throughout the changing weather conditions of our lives.

Conditions are changing in this country, the U.S. That is one reason to write about equanimity. I hope this piece supports you to recognize equanimity and develop it in your practice. Below, I describe two ways equanimity can appear, as well as some ways to develop it.

The Buddha often taught using images like the lighthouse I described. To my knowledge, he didn't speak about lighthouses in particular. But he did teach using similes of the ocean. He compared the sea to samsara, the vast and changing nature of life. The Buddha's famous phrase was "the ocean of existence."

Picture a lighthouse looking out over the ocean of existence. Coincidentally, the word for equanimity (upekkha) means "to look out over" in Pali, the language preserving the Buddha's teachings. In other words, to experience upekkha often means to take a wider view. This form of equanimity is often associated with meditation. It can be available in quiet moments of reflection as well.

A compound word also used for equanimity, tatramajjhattata, is quite a mouthful! One interpretation of its meaning is "to stand in the middle of things." This kind of equanimity is defined as keeping balance here and now. Imagine a lighthouse next to a stormy sea with huge waves splashing around it. Or surrounded by gusts of wind and big flocks of birds. Maybe these images convey the feeling of solidity and balance here and now, even in the storms of life. This is a complete form of equanimity too. It can feel quite different than a quiet look out over the bigger picture.

This kind of equanimity was helpful in my work as a hospital chaplain. Sometimes, I was called to the Emergency Room. Often, hectic activity and suffering would unfold all around. My role was to be "the calm in the storm." To stay balanced in the here and now. Moments when this is possible are moments of equanimity right in the middle of life's challenges.

To return to that lighthouse, it stands solid partly because it was built to be stable. What might not be as obvious is that it also rests upon a carefully laid foundation. If it were hastily built on shifting sand, it would collapse. It can be like that with qualities of mind cultivated through practice, too. If someone tries to make something happen fast without building a foundation in practice, it might not work out well. That is why there's so much teaching about cultivating foundations, or beneficial conditions, in Buddhist practice.

For example, if you try to hastily construct equanimity, you can accidentally cultivate indifference instead. Indifference is the near enemy of equanimity. In other words, indifference looks like equanimity, but can actually block it. This is one form of spiritual bypassing, a topic for another time. Like other forms of spiritual bypassing, indifference disconnects you from what is happening. Indifference can include apathy, shutdown, or internal resistance to your feelings.

Equanimity, on the other hand, encourages the heart and mind to be fully responsive. It allows you to be responsive and nonreactive. It is grounded in a sense of balance and perspective, rather than shutting down. It is a vital source of strength and resilience. Equanimity supports your capacity to respond wisely.

Meditation practitioners often confuse calm and equanimity. States of calm can feel blissful. They can be nourishing and beneficial in their own right. Calm itself, however, is not equanimity. There's a common situation for meditators in urban centers here, as well as in Asia, that reveals the difference.

On one daylong retreat, the meditation hall felt settled and silent. My meditation was quiet and calm. Then, the quietude collapsed. Nearby, street musicians arrived. They loudly serenaded everyone around with the same three songs, over and over. It went on for hours! Tension crept into my initial ease with the situation.

Later, after several cycles of song, and some cycles of internal commentary, equanimity emerged. My internal commentary dissolved. No trace of resistance remained. Instead, the mind felt cool and clear. It had no reaction at all. Those repetitive songs became a river of sound. Hearing was just another experience flowing through present moment awareness. This kind of unentangled awareness is a sure sign of equanimity. Taking things lightly is another sign: On that daylong retreat, things fell silent for a bit. Then, the music started up again. Instead of groans, the room erupted in laughter!

As these examples might suggest, equanimity is a simple and powerful quality. The Buddha praised it. His teachings place it among the most valued capacities a person can develop. And, it doesn't tend to work to try to quickly make equanimity happen. Enduring equanimity doesn't emerge on demand, any more than a long-lasting lighthouse can be hastily built on shifting sands. Instead, cultivating beneficial conditions creates a strong foundation for it. When equanimity emerges from gradually cultivating conditions, it will be strong and resilient.

Happily, mindfulness meditation practice naturally cultivates a solid foundation for equanimity. Here are some principles from a Buddhist perspective.

Keep practicing. The most important condition for cultivating equanimity is regular practice over time. Engaging with a teacher and community supports regular practice.

Stabilize your practice. Be intentional. Set other activities aside. Commit to each sit as a special time, and immerse yourself in meditation as best you can.

See obstacles as the path. In other words, when difficulty arises, turn toward it. Practice simple mindfulness. Turn toward what's tough with love. Doing so starts to build equanimity, bit by bit. In this way, the process echoes the goal. It builds capacity to be with all kinds of experience. Practice is like resistance training. It can be challenging! When challenges feel discouraging, it's often because of negative judgments about yourself or your meditation practice.

Set down harsh judgment. Many people have internalized a harsh or critical attitude. If critical judgments derail your meditation, you're not alone. Try not to be critical toward yourself for having judgments! Instead, cultivate helpful attitudes like kind interest, patience, and compassion. Notice what can improve, and do your best. When criticism comes, you might try an experiment. Imagine relating to your mind like a young, confused kid. Often our minds try to help by telling tall tales. It's possible to be kind without believing the story! Met with mindful kindness and skepticism, unhelpful judgments can dissolve. Or, better yet, evolve into discernment.

Discern what's helpful and what isn't. Harshly criticizing yourself or your experience isn't helpful. It is crucial, however, to discern between mental actions leading to benefit versus harm. The art of cultivating equanimity includes some discernment, or wisdom. The first act of discernment can be to step back from what's going on. Then, the mind becomes less seduced by thinking. Discernment increases. Then, it becomes easier to disengage from thought patterns that increase suffering.

Discernment increases capacity to notice and cultivate beneficial qualities like equanimity.

Get curious, and stay interested! Curiosity about the process of meditation energizes practice. It gives your mind something useful to do here and now. Relaxed interest also helps to increase discernment, which supports mature practice, including equanimity. It's especially helpful to be interested in your response to moments of difficulty and moments of ease.

Appreciate moments of contentment. Contentment contributes to equanimity. Don't underestimate its power! Learning to be content weakens the habitual outward reach for happiness. In contrast, contentment supports a simple happiness of being present. A powerful condition for increasing contentment is to value it.

Trust. Another supportive condition for cultivating equanimity is to trust meditation practice. Meditation works like a gradual exercise regimen, not a miracle pill. It takes time. Trust the process. Cultivate confidence based on your teacher, books, or your own small wins. Trust and confidence support the maturation of practice, including equanimity.

Finally, equanimity can emerge through intentionally contemplating a wider perspective. A lighthouse looks out over the enormous ocean, including boats, animals, tides, and weather systems. In the same way, taking in the big picture can develop equanimity. This can include recollecting immense lengths of time, the vast variety of living beings, and the many conditions that influence each of us. Standing *in this simple moment* while taking in the larger view can remind us not to take things so personally. Not taking things personally is perhaps the core of equanimity. It is also an expression of maturity in Buddhist practice.

As equanimity matures, it strengthens and nurtures wisdom. To return to our starting simile, the lighthouse's light turns on. And that light of wisdom can guide each person through the ocean of existence.

Dawn Neal is the Guiding Teacher for Insight Santa Cruz, teaches a regular group for IMC, and serves as core faculty for the Sati Center for Buddhist Studies Online Buddhist Chaplaincy Training Program. Dawn holds an MA from the Institute of Buddhist Studies and Graduate Theological Union. Prior to teaching Dharma full time, she was an Interfaith Spiritual Care professional (Chaplain) at Stanford Medicine.

The Parami of Wisdom

Francisco Morillo Gable

When the Parami of Wisdom was introduced to me in chaplaincy training at the Sati Center 11 years ago, I had a vague notion of wisdom that had to do with philosophical and moral ideals.

Gil Fronsdal's adaptation of *A Treatise on the Paramis* presents wisdom as a process of seeing clearly the end of suffering:

> Wisdom has the characteristic of penetrating the real specific nature (of phenomena); its function is to illuminate the objective field, like a lamp, with knowledge that restores sight. ... Through wisdom one aspires to nibbana. ... Through wisdom and compassion one becomes one's own protector and the protector of others.

During my training internship at Sojourn Chaplaincy in San Francisco General, I was learning to provide pastoral care to patients in stages of dis-ease and death, while also dealing with my own physical pain from a spinal disability. I was doing this with professional chaplains whose clear religious conviction I lacked. My internship gave me a big push to try understanding this Parami.

Rather than intellectual or moral elevation, what I've been finding these many years—with an increasing crescendo of faith—is a practice of "noble care."

Glimpses of Hidden Realities

The wisdom in the Parami comes from insight in mindfulness meditation. Insight is contemplation with the mind's eye, not our physical eyes. It's an internal way of observing that combines both knowing and sensing, along with relaxing. To arrive at this lush layering of sensory information we train in knowing the body in the body—we train in experiencing it, and relaxing it. We also train with feeling tones, the mind, and its activities. This fills us with reflexive awareness and insight.

Insight in mindfulness of thinking, for instance, is a glimpse into the hidden nature of thoughts. We develop sensory knowledge about thoughts, which includes thoughts' physicality, energy, attitude, and motivation. That sensory knowledge about thoughts loosens the tight grip of discursive thinking. It highlights how the defilements of greed, hate, and delusion manufacture thoughts that lead to cycles of suffering. We learn what to steer away from.

We also discover that observation of any object of mindfulness dismantles unhelpful mental and bodily activities. What our heart needs most can then come to the surface.

Accomplishment in Virtue

Wholesome feelings from our ethical virtue and samadhi trainings bolster sensory knowledge that gives us wisdom about suffering.

In Buddhism, ethics are not followed for moralistic reasons, as if commanded by a lawgiver. In this tradition, we are the arbiters. Supported by mindfulness, we reflect and deliberate in order to behave in conscientious ways with the overarching principle of "do no harm." Sexual violence, for instance, is always unethical because it causes significant harm. Being ethical is a sensitivity that comes from a purity of the heart that does no harm.

Our society organizes itself around the defilements to a relatively high degree, I think, and we inherit some of this perspective through our upbringing. Buddhism offers an ethical framework to nurture ethical maturation that takes profound attention and devotion to practice. Our sensitivity gets developed through the energy movements of mindfulness and insight. The fruits of devoted practice are peace, security, and the "bliss of the blamelessness."

The tradition calls these wholesome feelings that come from practice unworldly (niramisa in Pali). They are non-sensual and free of defilements. What the *Treatise* calls "accomplishment in virtue" is an all-encompassing sensibility for non-harming that removes traces of uncertainty about what's wholesome. It builds our capacity for discernment and our faith in the Dharma.

Tranquility

In samadhi practice, wholesome feelings fill us with energy that heals and provides momentum and clarity.

Anytime that we can shift away from our suffering, or dukkha, and have faith to find ease, we experience healing reassurance. In that simple but not always easy movement, we no longer identify with dukkha. We've started to steer away from the chain of reactions that created the dukkha (e.g., clinging, craving, and compulsions of reactivity). Like grace, a biological momentum comes forth with tranquility that we may need and can receive. It may be compassion, benevolence, or a type of joy and happiness that has a caring spaciousness that settles and lifts us.

Samadhi (a form of tranquility in early Buddhism) grows by receiving these feelings and releasing obstructions. As the hindrances go into abeyance, samadhi increases with states of stable stillness. The knots that fragment the mind-heart begin to clear, and we become absorbed in sensory contact.

Breathing, for example, can be felt without the usual concept of "breath," instead being felt as a harmonious series of movements such as expansion, tautness, pressure, jaggedness, and softness. Singleness of attention comes to the fore. This can establish some of the highest states of joy, happiness, and equanimity. To me, this feels like soaking in hot springs in winter and identifying with the sunlight currents reflecting in the flat surface when the mud has settled.

Samadhi provides a medium of safety for our mindfulness to feel profoundly at home in our being and the clarity for insight to blossom.

Knowledge of the Way Things Are

The radical insight the Buddhist tradition calls "knowledge and vision of the way things are" penetrates through the three characteristics of impermanence, suffering, and not-self into emptiness. This insight arrives at the absence of suffering. This tradition emphasizes how suffering gets produced and how it ends—a high form of care.

Mindfulness of sensory experience that is engrossing can connect us with the miracle of life's movement and show us that everything is in constant flux. Since everything is beginning and ending all the time, there is nothing to cling to. Any clinging is suffering.

The one who experiences change (me, myself, I) is also perceived as coming and going, and we find it is empty of a permanent self, with all of its ideas and views. Intimacy with sense experience lets us appreciate how perceptions create bigger threads of concepts and stories.

At the end of ignorance we see that attachment to sensual pleasure, to views, and to self can keep one trapped in small worlds of incessant repetitive spinning. In an old African legend, a saltwater fish that lives in a fish bowl carved out of wood is one day released into a tide pool by the sea. Astonishingly, it only makes circles in the same size as the bowl. Why not swim away free?

Our attachment to me, myself, and I can get fixated on the roles of society's collective theater, spinning limiting narratives around in a fish bowl.

However, it's possible to know and sense release and to recognize there are no edges to concepts made by our mind. To be free, we're first mindful of how we get caught, and then we're wise and we take the medicine of letting go. Otherwise, attachments get the upper hand.

Final liberation is cessation of the world created by the six senses, which we have made with what we see, hear, smell, taste, feel with the body, and know in the mind. This is much easier with the ethical certainty that safeguarding the sense doors is the same as being a caretaker for our inner being.

Liberation is the courage to go with the stream that flows into a calm signless nothingness that is not nothing. A heart that's free of blemish and full of the bliss of blamelessness is phenomenal.

Final liberation is release—release into non-greed, non-hatred, and non-delusion; release into love, maturity, and body-fullness. Release is fearless self-emptying love. The deathless that is nirvana is complete fearlessness. Barriers dissolve, sublime security dawns: the fish joins the currents of the sea.

Self-Emptying Love

Liberation, however, is not the end of the story in the Treatise, even when our subjectivity is safely anchored while letting go of I-making, even when the manufacturing of mental worlds ceases in states of awakening. There is yet more. The supreme form of care is knowledge of liberation. It's the maturity to know how to get out of suffering, to not pick up attachments, and to not ignore encumbrances. It's the faith to be open to the grace of samadhi.

That which remains then is to care for others. Compassion and wisdom go hand-in-hand in the Treatise. The Buddha modeled this for us after his final awakening: he turned toward, not away from its suffering. He worked untiringly out of care for others' salvation from dukkha.

The Buddha also urged us to go forth for the good of this world. To go forth in this holy life is to turn to the world while unstintingly doing the practice. Practice reminds me of learning to play the oboe in childhood. There were infinite scales to learn, forever it seemed, and then there was the repetitive execution of notes into melodies—until one "magical" day there was something called music. Music, for the amateur who's a lover of craft, is continuous practice; it's a practice that becomes a cycle of fulfillment.

May we keep seeking and trusting in the reassurance of our Dharma practice.

Francisco Morillo Gable is a classically trained Dharma Teacher. He was born and raised in the Dominican Republic until the age of 10. He studied Comparative Literature and minored in West African Dance at UCLA.

Meditate Like the Earth

Kirsten Rudestam

The birds have vanished down the sky.
Now the last cloud drains away.
We sit together, the mountain and me,
until only the mountain remains.

—*Li Bai*

One of my earliest memories is of being in a double stroller next to my twin sister. My mother handed each of us a stick of a Kit Kat bar. I ate mine right away, but my sister held hers tightly in her tiny fist, gazing up at it in fascination as it began to melt down her arm. Tormented with desire for her chocolate, I remember pleading with her, "Eat it, Monica! Eat it!!" If only her Kit Kat bar would disappear, I could be freed from the excruciating experience of wanting it.

It's a cute story—a toddler obsessed with the desire for something she can't have and her recognition that without the sight of it she would be freed of the pain of wanting it. But there's also something sobering about the pain of longing for something so much that little me couldn't simply sit with the empathetic joy of watching my sister enjoy her candy in her own way. That pain was and is real, and it points to one of the central teachings of the Buddha—that we suffer when we want things to be other than they are.

I love the simple wisdom in this truth, and I also love the teachings associated with it. The Buddha didn't instruct us to run away or turn from suffering; instead, he encouraged us to stay close and intimate, to investigate and learn from the pain of wanting and pushing away. This process of investigation requires many things, including courage, faith, compassion, and mindfulness. It also requires patience.

Khanti is the sixth of the ten paramis, those noble qualities or virtues that are foundational trainings in the teachings and practice of Buddhism. While most often translated as patience, khanti is also likened to forbearance, persistence, endurance, and acceptance. As we acknowledge the presence of something painful, khanti helps us to stay with it and to not wiggle, manipulate, blame, or react. Instead, this parami is foundational in cultivating a heart that can stay steady when life does not accommodate our wishes.

A handful of years ago, I set out on a solo backpacking trip in the Sierras. After a hot, bright day of hiking, I reached the place I wanted to camp for the night, hastily set up my tent, and then, eager to explore without weight on my back, started scampering up the granite rock lining a dry creek bed. I had changed out my running shoes for a pair of sandals and went empty-handed, planning to turn around after not too long. But there is nothing so compelling as a dry wash snaking its way through ponderosa and cottonwoods, and I found myself an hour later perched at the top of a set of boulders, gazing out at the quiet expanse of mountains dotted with silver lakes and swaths of green pine amid the grey rock.

My reverie was interrupted by a rumble, and I turned to see dark clouds assembling in the distance. Minutes later, the sky opened up above and sheets of rain began pouring down, plastering my clothes to my body. Making my way back to the tent, I was soaked and shivering, eager to get into a dry space and change into warm clothes. But when I got back to camp, I was horrified to find my tent flooded. All I could do was sit in a puddle of water, arms wrapped around my legs, waiting for the storm to end.

And that storm took its time, transitioning to hail and then back to rain, and then to hail again. Every few minutes, I peered out from under the rainfly to see if I could find a gap in the clouds. Each time, seeing nothing but rain, hail, and swells of dark clouds, my heart sank. I felt defeated and miserable. After a while of this waiting, looking, and suffering, my mind saw how much extra agitation I was adding to the experience by anxiously waiting for a break in the rain. I began laughing out loud at the absurdity of the situation—it was so unpleasant! And yet in the moment of seeing and feeling the reactivity, the impatient mind softened. The storm blew by in just the amount of time it took for it to arrive. I continued to feel damp and cold, but these sensations were accompanied by loving kindness and humor rather than aversion—a much more spacious and easeful experience! This is all to say, when we try to outrun suffering, we just find ourselves hurting more.

How often do we feel compelled to move quickly, to get things done in the least amount of time so that we can get the next thing done in the least amount of time? We may notice that the contracted, rushed mind rarely rests. The momentum of leaning forward carries through, even after crossing all the items off of our to-do list.

Impatience has been a long-time habit of mine. Once, a friend and I went for a bicycle ride to pick up some groceries in town. As we rode, I asked him some questions about his work. He had founded a nonprofit organization, which he called Take Back Your Time, that aimed to discourage what he saw as a cultural tendency to prioritize productivity above rest and consumption above sufficiency.

"What kind of things do you actually teach or recommend?" I asked. As we approached a traffic light turning from green to yellow, I instinctively pedaled faster to make it through the intersection before it turned red. My friend, however, stopped at the yellow light, and I was forced to slow down in order to wait for him on the other side of the street. When he met up with me, he answered my question, "Well, for example, like that. When you're not in a rush, don't be in a rush."

We need patience not only to help us bear that which is difficult or unpleasant, like sitting in a rainstorm, but also to help us decondition the very root of restlessness that pushes us to lean forward into the next moment, no matter how satisfying the current moment may be. Standing in line, driving in traffic, listening to the same story over again, sitting in the waiting room of a doctor's office—all of these can be considered teachers of patience. We can connect with the part that is restless, that clenches inside as if tightening against the moment. We can take these as opportunities to cultivate the parami of khanti and remind ourselves that life is lived, experienced, loved, right here and now.

Cultivating patience requires trust, and perhaps most beautiful of all, it requires letting go. It's common to have an agenda, conscious or not, for how we want and expect our practice to unfold. If the mind is busy, we may long for it to settle; we may be eager for insight to emerge, for our hearts to be clear of greed, hatred, and delusion. It can be skillful to hold an intention for practice, but fundamentally we are not able to control the course of our spiritual unfolding.

The Buddha described this as a gradual path; causes and conditions ripen, and we are tasked not with making things happen, but with responding with the clarity and acceptance that is available to us in each moment. Fundamental to the quality of patience is this process of letting go. We are asked to surrender our ideas of how and when we would like things to happen. We allow the chocolate to melt and the clouds to shed the last of their rain. We allow life to run its own course.

There is one great teacher of patience that is with us always, and that is this wide, steady earth. This earth that moves at its own pace, where everything unfolds, seeds, sprouts, and grows on its own time. The sun moving in its unhurried arc across the sky each day; the days that darken and lengthen according to their own rhythms; and the earth holding it all, so enduring and unconditionally accepting. We can receive the lesson that the Buddha taught his son Rahula when he advised him to "meditate like the earth." When we meditate like the earth, we may receive a taste of this grounded quality of patience and discover our own capacity to let go and to trust life. We may go beyond a need for patience at all, as without a desire for things to change, patience itself becomes obsolete.

Kirsten Rudestam has been practicing meditation in the Theravadan tradition since 2001 and serves as core faculty for the Sati Center's Buddhist Eco-Chaplaincy training program. She holds a PhD in Environmental Sociology and is a long-time student and teacher of environmental justice and earth-based practices. When not exploring water-bodies or on retreat, she lives in a yurt in White Salmon, Washington.

The Art of Waiting: Cultivating Patience on the Path

Mei Elliott

While walking through the flower garden at Green Gulch Farm and Zen Center, I ran into my old friend Kogen and his four-year-old daughter, Caliope. Kogen and I had trained as monks together at Tassajara years before, and it was heartening to see him now as a father. Caliope, small and bright-eyed, dug around in a nearby flower bed while we caught up. Unfortunately, this didn't hold her interest, and it wasn't long before she started tugging on her dad's pant leg signaling it was time to go. As her impatience grew, her easy mood unravelled until her frustration bordered on a tantrum. Yet, to my surprise, Kogen remained kind and gentle with her. His voice was soft and reassuring as he knelt beside her. Amazed by his steadiness and composure, I finally asked, "How do you do it, Kogen? How are you so patient?"

Kogen raised an eyebrow and smiled wryly. "You don't know what it's like in here," he replied, referencing his world within.

The Buddha described patience as the highest virtue, yet few of us fully understand what patience truly is or how to cultivate it. Kogen's graceful restraint demonstrated patient activity: the capacity to engage calmly with his daughter, even amid his inner frustration. This is a remarkable skill—one that shields others from the brunt of our own discomfort—and yet, we're often at a loss when it comes to calming the impatience that simmers in our own heart. Growing up, parents and teachers repeatedly request patience from their children but don't provide instruction. Meanwhile, we're the ones who often need these instructions most.

By one definition, patience is "the capacity to accept or tolerate delay, trouble, or suffering without getting angry or upset." It is the ability to bear difficulty calmly, and to be steadfast despite adversity. One of my Zen teachers used to say, "The first element of patience is a willingness to suffer," which is fitting, given that patience comes from the Latin "pati," which bears this very meaning—to suffer. In being patient we are willing to rest in difficulty.

One common misassociation with patience is that it involves gritting our teeth and bearing our circumstance. But true patience isn't the tightening and clenching that takes place as we run through a storm. Rather, patience is the willingness to allow difficulty. It's the ability to be with what is, while maintaining a wholesome attitude. Patience can allow us to walk in a cold rain, without rushing, with the body relaxed. In this way, patience can become an umbrella during times of challenge. Without it, we often find ourselves rushing through our life.

It's no surprise, then, that the universal refrain of impatience is, "Are we there yet?" Like children, we sit in the backseat of our life, ignoring the passing landscapes: the red rocks of Arizona, the snowcaps of the Rockies—and instead are so fixated on getting to the hotel pool that we miss the beauty of the journey, which is none other than our life. Yes, the car is hot and stuffy, we're a little queasy, and our little brother is making farting noises with his armpit. Understandably, it's hard to enjoy the view. And yet it's patience that can help us bear the gap. Ultimately, it's patience that can help us meet the only life we have.

How, then, do we cultivate patience? The path begins by studying its opposite—impatience. Though impatience is a frequent visitor for many of us, it's not always clear what it is or how it functions. When we take a closer look, what we find is that impatience always comes along with a companion: craving or aversion. Impatience arises in tandem with desire and dislike, with our wanting and not wanting. We could say that impatience and craving walk hand-in-hand.

When something obstructs us from obtaining what we want—whether it's a cup of coffee, a bathroom break, or a better job—impatience quickly takes hold. We typically want rapid and unhindered access to that which we desire, and if anything gets between us and what we want, impatience reigns supreme.

Likewise, when we experience something unpleasant, something we don't want—pain in the body, an illness, a dismal mood, sadness, or loss—impatience urges us to rush through it. In both cases, when desire or aversion is present, impatience often tags along like a shadow.

Like most shadows, which generally go unnoticed, we typically aren't even aware when impatience is present. So our first task is simply recognizing impatience when it comes to visit. When we start this study, it can be surprising how pervasive impatience can be; it appears while driving in traffic, during conversations with others, when stuck with a slow internet connection, or while waiting in line at the grocery. We prefer to burn our tongues rather than wait for our coffee to cool down. When impatience is present, whether it's mild or strong, our task is to see it with clear recognition.

As humbling as our impatience is, these minor-league occasions provide opportunities to grow the muscle of patience before it's needed in more difficult circumstances. We can't expect patience to be present in hardship if we haven't cultivated it with lesser challenges. In order to be able to patiently endure the most devastating difficulties—a terminal illness, the grief that comes in response to the loss of loved ones—we need to start small. If we want to be able to lift a 100 lb. dumbbell, we need to start by lifting a 5 lb. weight.

Having recognized impatience, our next task is to study what it feels like within us. What does it feel like physically? Is there a tightness in the chest, a clenched jaw, or heat in the face? We can become interested in impatience, getting to know it in the same way we might study a museum exhibit. Through our continued curiosity, we become more adept at sensing impatience when it arrives, and thereby we become less likely to become possessed by it.

Once we recognize impatience and feel it in the body, we can call on wisdom and compassion, which provide important nourishment for patience. We can lean into wisdom by remembering that all things pass. Nothing lasts forever. This mood, this pain, this circumstance will eventually end. And in the meantime, even as it seems to persist, the experience of it is inconstant—it ebbs and flows in intensity. What might seem static at first, when we look more closely, actually varies and changes. Seeing these subtle changes can begin to dissolve our fixed perception of the circumstance. Knowing this, we can relax into things as they are. When we realize how quickly things pass—and that they pass on their own, without our volition—we stop leaning as eagerly into the future. In this way, patience emerges as a product of clear seeing, of wisdom.

Likewise, compassion softens patience with its warmth. In the same way that Kogen knelt beside his daughter, we can meet our own impatience with gentleness and kindness. We can direct this comforting compassion toward the child within us—the vulnerable part of ourselves that longs for things to be otherwise. When we bring compassion to the impatient being within, the warmth of kindness can begin to soften our resistance. Sometimes this softening can reveal that impatience is covering up deeper hurts. We might find that below our impatience, emotions like sadness, loneliness, or grief are asking for our loving attention.

So we start small, bringing wisdom and compassion to our minor difficulties. Then, when something significant comes along, we're more ready, more steady, more able to meet it. I sometimes bring to mind Nelson Mandela, who spent 27 years incarcerated, much of it on Robben Island where he lived with harsh conditions and isolation. He was allowed to have one visitor a year for a 30-minute period and could exchange no more than one letter every six months.

Despite the severe limitations on his freedom, Mandela remained steadfast, relating to his imprisonment as an education in patience and perseverance. Whatever difficulty we find ourselves in, we too can meet it as an education in patience. We all have the capacity to remain equanimous amid even the greatest hardships.

When we meet our difficult circumstances with this patient nobility, we're not the only ones who benefit. Our children, our coworkers, and everyone we encounter can benefit from our peace.

This peace doesn't require perfection. We can learn to meet ourselves where we're at; we can recognize the pattern of impatience, getting to know when it visits and how it feels. In doing so, we open the door for wisdom and compassion to free the heart. Over time, we can even learn to be patient with impatience itself.

It's said that the Dalai Lama was once asked, "What is the fastest way to enlightenment?" He replied, "Patience."

When we're faced with crossing the great flood of samsara, patience can provide us with a raft and a sail. And when patience is mature, we might even enjoy the voyage.

Mei Elliott practices in both the Theravada and Zen traditions. She trained as a Zen monk at Tassajara Zen Center and spent eight years living at Zen temples and monasteries. Mei was authorized to teach through IMC and currently resides at Insight Retreat Center in Santa Cruz, CA, where she serves as the Co-Managing Director.

Dedication

This book is dedicated to Gil Fronsdal and Andrea Fella by the 15 new IMC teachers whose voices fill its pages. Warm hand to warm hand, the Dharma flows in all directions. Having received the warmth of this training, we joyously offer it back to our teachers and outward to the world.

About IMC

The Insight Meditation Center (IMC) is dedicated to the study and practice of Buddhist ideals—mindfulness, ethics, compassion, loving-kindness, and liberation. At the heart of all IMC activities is the practice of Insight Meditation, sometimes called mindfulness or vipassana meditation. Based on a 2500-year-old Buddhist teaching, this practice helps us to see more deeply and clearly into our lives. With insight, we develop ways of living more peacefully, compassionately, and wisely. Daily practice is integral to Insight practice: both daily meditation practice, and the practice of mindfulness and compassion as we go about our daily lives. From this foundation in meditation and mindfulness, IMC actively seeks to support practitioners in integrating and applying their spiritual life in all areas of life.

Made in USA - Kendallville, IN
59628_9780984509232
02.24.2025 2025